Funded by a State Legislature Grant
Senator Suzi Oppenheimer

RYE FREE READING ROOM
Escape to the Library

Bloom's

GUIDES

Erich Maria Remarque's
All Quiet on the Western Front

CURRENTLY AVAILABLE

The Adventures of
Huckleberry Finn
All Quiet on the Western Front
All the Pretty Horses
Animal Farm
The Autobiography of Malcolm X
The Awakening
Beloved
Beowulf
Brave New World
The Canterbury Tales
The Catcher in the Rye
The Chosen
The Crucible
Cry, the Beloved Country
Death of a Salesman
Fahrenheit 451
Frankenstein
The Glass Menagerie
The Grapes of Wrath
Great Expectations
The Great Gatsby
Hamlet
The Handmaid's Tale
The House on Mango Street
I Know Why the Caged Bird Sings
The Iliad
Invisible Man
Jane Eyre

Lord of the Flies
Macbeth
Maggie: A Girl of the Streets
The Member of the Wedding
The Metamorphosis
Native Son
1984
The Odyssey
Oedipus Rex
Of Mice and Men
One Hundred Years of Solitude
Pride and Prejudice
Ragtime
The Red Badge of Courage
Romeo and Juliet
The Scarlet Letter
A Separate Peace
Slaughterhouse-Five
Snow Falling on Cedars
The Stranger
A Streetcar Named Desire
The Sun Also Rises
A Tale of Two Cities
The Things They Carried
To Kill a Mockingbird
Uncle Tom's Cabin
The Waste Land
Wuthering Heights

Bloom's
GUIDES

Erich Maria Remarque's
All Quiet on the Western Front

Edited & with an Introduction
by Harold Bloom

BLOOM'S
LITERARY CRITICISM
An imprint of Infobase Publishing

Bloom's Guides: All Quiet on the Western Front

Bloom's Literary Criticism
An imprint of Infobase Publishing
132 West 31st Street
New York NY 10001

Library of Congress Cataloging-in-Publication Data
Bloom, Harold.
   Erich Maria Remarque's All quiet on the western front / Harold Bloom.
      p. cm. — (Bloom's guides)
   Includes bibliographical references and index.
   ISBN 978-0-7910-9830-1 (hardcover)
   1. Remarque, Erich Maria, 1898–1970. Im Westen nichts Neues.
I. Title. II. Title: All quiet on the western front. III. Series.

   PT2635.E68I664 1984
   833'.912—dc22

                              2008001209

Contributing Editor: Janyce Marson
Cover design by Takeshi Takahashi
Printed in the United States of America
Bang EJB 10 9 8 7 6 5 4 3 2 1
This book is printed on acid-free paper.

Contents

 Introduction

HAROLD BLOOM

All Quiet on the Western Front was first published in book form in 1929, and was translated soon after into English. It was Erich Maria Remarque's third novel, and has always remained his most popular, though several of his later works were very successful with the public in the 1940s and 1950s. But his other books have faded away, and now are scarcely readable. *All Quiet on the Western Front* remains very popular and is widely read, but whether it is more than another period piece seems quite questionable to me.

As a literary critic I have always tried to follow Dr. Samuel Johnson, who warned that contemporary literary fame has a way of vanishing:

> Of many writers who filled their age with wonder, and whose names we find celebrated in the books of their contemporaries, the works are now no longer to be seen, or are seen only amidst the lumber of libraries which are seldom visited, where they lie only to show the deceitfulness of hope, and the uncertainty of honour.
>
> Of the decline of reputation many causes may be assigned. It is commonly lost because it never was deserved, and was conferred at first, not by the suffrage of criticism, but by the fondness of friendship, or servility of flattery. The great and popular are very freely applauded, but all soon grow weary of echoing to each other a name which has no other claim to notice, but that many mouths are pronouncing it at once.

Let me add, to the great Samuel Johnson, the sublime Oscar Wilde with his two critical adages: everything matters in art, except the subject, and all bad literature is sincere. What matters most in *All Quiet on the Western Front* indeed is the subject,

7

World War I, and the book is very sincere. It is therefore not a work of art, but a period piece and a historical document.

To be even more autobiographical, I discovered recently how much fury can be generated by naming a currently popular work as just another period piece. After I discussed the Harry Potter fad in the *Wall Street Journal*, the *Journal* received eighty negative letters and none positive. J. K. Rowling, like Stephen King and Danielle Steele, will join the thousands of other writers in "the lumber of libraries" and the dustbin of the ages. Popularity is an index to popularity, and to nothing more.

Remarque's *All Quiet on the Western Front*, still popular, remains an effective enough anti-war tract, but it hardly competes with Hemingway's *A Farewell to Arms* or even with Norman Mailer's *The Naked and the Dead*. Though Remarque's style is terse and tense, his protagonist lacks significant personality or mind to be of lasting interest to the reader. Paul Bäumer doubtless was meant to be a kind of everyman, but he is as drab as he is desperate, and his yearnings are too commonplace to be interesting. Lew Ayres, playing Paul Bäumer in the American film version (1931), invested the character with more integrity and stubborn honor than Remarque had been able to suggest.

Remarque's novel is narrated by Bäumer in the first person. It is ironic that the book's most effective paragraphs are the final ones, in which Bäumer's voice ceases, and we are glad to receive a third-person narration though it be of the young man's death:

He fell in October 1918, on a day that was so quiet and still on the whole front, that the army report confined itself to the single sentence: All quiet on the Western Front.

He had fallen forward and lay on the earth as though sleeping. Turning him over one saw that he could not have suffered long; his face had an expression of calm, as though almost glad the end had come.

Biographical Sketch

Erich Remarque was born on June 22, 1898, in Osnabrück, Germany, to a Catholic family of French ancestry. His father, Peter Franz Remark, a bookbinder, was generally gruff and uncommunicative, and his mother, Anna Maria Stallknecht, was an attractive but frail woman who had suffered the death of a son at the age of six in 1901 when Erich was three years old. She always harbored a strong desire for Erich to become a teacher. In 1904 Remarque began his education at two Catholic schools, first at the Domschule primary school in 1904 and then at the Johannisschule, where he first enrolled in 1908. Remarque was a good student, although resistant to the rigors of religious education. At the Johannisschule, he joined the church choir, an activity that would influence his lifelong love of music. It was there that he also developed a deep love for literature. By the time he entered the Katholische Präparande in 1912, where he embarked on a three-year course to prepare for admission to the Catholic Teachers' Seminar, he was reading such authors as Goethe, Dostoevsky, Hermann Hesse, Jack London, Thomas Mann, Schopenhauer, and Rilke. From 1915 to 1916, Remarque attended the Catholic Teachers' Seminar to train for a career as an elementary schoolteacher. This is also where he became involved with a group of students who referred to themselves as the Traumbude Circle (*traumbude* meaning "dream room" or "den of dreams"). The Traumbude Circle was a forum devoted to the discussion and admiration of the art nouveau movement known as the Jugenstil. Equally as important at this time was Remarque's friendship with the group's leader, Fritz Hörstemeier, a man twice Remarque's age, who gave his young protégé support and encouragement. Remarque would later look back on this time in his life with great fondness.

On November 16, 1916, Remarque was drafted into the army along with other classmates from the Catholic Teachers' Seminar. The group received basic training at the Caprivi Barracks, named for Bismarck's successor, on the outskirts of Osnabrück. During this phase of his training, Remarque was able to make frequent visits back home to see his dying mother. On June 12, 1917, Remarque's company was sent to France and, shortly thereafter, he was sent to Belgium where he was assigned trench duty near Houthulst Forest with his school friend, George Middendorf, working beside him. In July, Remarque was wounded and taken to a nearby hospital in Tourout, then was transferred in August to St. Vincenz Hospital in Duisburg, Germany. In September, Remarque's mother died, followed a half year later by the death of his mentor, Fritz Hörtstemeier, on March 6, 1918. Later that year, Remarque published some sentimental poetry in the avant-garde journal, *Die Schönheit*. In October, he was released from St. Vincenz Hospital and transferred to a reserve unit in Osnabrück. He returned to active duty in November. When World War I ended, Remarque was discharged during a period of great social and political upheaval throughout Germany, given that the terms of peace with the Allies were particularly severe. Under the Treaty of Versailles, signed on June 28, 1919, Germany and its allies had to accept full responsibility for causing the war and make substantial territorial concessions and pay reparations to certain effected nations.

In June 1919 Remarque passed the teacher's examination and was then hired as a substitute teacher in Lohne. At this time, he also continued to write music and art criticism for the local Osnabrück newspapers. In 1920 he wrote his first novel, *The Dream Room*. Remarque continued writing, moving on to a second teaching position in the small village of Klein Berssen, Hummling. Remarque's third teaching position took him to Nahne, a town near his native Osnabrück, where he successfully completed his work and then asked to be dismissed. Following this final teaching post, Remarque moved from one miscellaneous job to the next for the next two years, working as a salesman, a store engraver, and as an organist at an Osnabrück mental-health facility. Following these various jobs, Remarque moved to Hannover and became the editor and publicity director for the Continental Rubber Company. There he created a popular cartoon hero named Hein (Captain

Hein Priemke) for a series he produced. Beyond its obvious remunerative value, this last job was significant for it was in this professional setting that Remarque discovered his true creative and fictional skills while writing and editing advertising copy. In 1925 Remarque made another decisive move when he took up residence in Berlin, the publishing capital of Germany. He became the picture editor for *Sport im Bild* newspaper, a publication of Scherl Verlag whose target audience was car owners and racecar drivers. While living in Berlin, Remarque met many musicians, people associated with the theater, and movie stars and, in all likelihood, met Marlene Dietrich for the first time, though it would be approximately ten years before they would see each other again. On October 14, 1925, Remarque married Jutta Ilse Zambona, a minor actress and dancer Remarque had met in Hannover. Jutta was demanding and prone to erratic behavior. Remarque embarked on a turbulent relationship with a woman who would soon prove unfaithful herself, a revelation that caused him great despair. In 1927, his domestic circumstances notwithstanding, Remarque began to funnel his energy into writing *All Quiet on the Western Front*, and, in the early months of 1928, he reluctantly submitted his manuscript to several prestigious Berlin publishing houses.

All Quiet was rejected by the house of S. Fischer Verlag, the publisher of Thomas Mann's *Buddenbrooks*, apparently because Samuel Fischer was skeptical about the public's continued interest in World War I. The book was eventually accepted by Propyläen Verlag, the book division of the enormous Ullstein publishing house, with the stipulation that it first be serialized in Ullstein's newspaper, the liberal *Die Vossiche Zeitung*. Remarque's signature novel appeared in serial form from November 10 to December 9 of that year, followed by its release in book form on January 31, 1929. As a result of its publication, Remarque created a political firestorm in which he became a source of contention for the right, a disappointment to the left, and a well-known literary figure for his growing readership, which in turn lead to his great success and financial gain. From this time forward, "Remarque" became the adopted spelling of his surname, replacing the previously used Remark. A year later, on January 4, 1930, Remarque divorced Jutta Ilsa Zambona though they continued to occupy the same Berlin apartment and were still seen together at fashionable restaurants. Despite their several divorces and estrangements in the ensuing years, Jutta would continue to play an influential role in Remarque's life.

Sometime in late January 1933, following Hitler's takeover of Germany, Erich Maria Remarque escaped Nazi Germany, taking Jutta Zambona with him to Switzerland. By the time he fled Germany, Remarque had already published, in 1933, the sequel to *All Quiet on the Western Front*, titled *The Road Back*. Remarque was also extremely lucky in having escaped with his life. A few months later, on March 29, 1933, following Nazi aggression against "internationalism and Judaism," seven copies of *All Quiet on the Western Front* were consigned to the flames along with many other "undesirable" books. Then on May 10, thousands of books were burned at the Operplatz by nine designated students. With Joseph Goebbels arriving to fan the flames, both literally and rhetorically, howling mobs continued to arrive on the scene, dancing and hurling invectives as books were continually fed into the enormous pyre. Though anguished to be alienated from his country, he had left Germany just in time, having previously made contingency plans to live elsewhere. A few years earlier, in an effort to get away from an increasingly tense political situation in Berlin, Remarque traveled a great deal and, in 1931, purchased a beautiful three-story villa in Switzerland in the popular Lake Maggiore area of Porto Ronco. He hired Joseph and Rosa Kramer as gardener and housekeeper, respectively, and the couple would remain his faithful servants, protecting his home throughout World War II. On January 22, 1938, Remarque married Jutta for a second time in a token ceremony in St. Mortiz, his motivation being a genuine concern for Jutta's political predicament as he was afraid she might lose her residency permit in Switzerland, which in turn could have lead to her deportation to Nazi Germany. Even more ominous was the fact that during this time Remarque learned that the Gestapo was compiling a report on him, replete with false accusations that he had insulted the memory of German soldiers in World War I and had demonstrated sympathy for Jews and communists. In July 1938 Remarque was expatriated by the Nazis and, in November, Jutta was likewise stripped of citizenship. In response to the radical transformation occurring in Germany, Remarque wrote *Flotsam* with the inscription that read: "To live without roots takes a stout heart."

In March 1939, observing the Nazi takeover of much of Europe, Remarque decided to go to the United States. He arrived in New York City on a foggy morning on March 23. It was the same day that Hitler annexed the former German Baltic port city of Memel and Neville Chamberlain warned the Führer against any attempt at world domination. Remarque was charmed by the sights and attractions of New York City, including the Empire State Building and his suite at the Waldorf-Astoria. Marlene Dietrich contacted him soon after his arrival, and Remarque was soon headed for Los Angeles. Once in Hollywood, Remarque was living the high life with such celebrities as Gary Cooper, Errol Flynn, Ronald Colman, Douglas Fairbanks Jr., and Dolores del Rio, with whom he became romantically involved for a brief time. During a brief trip to Switzerland in the summer of 1939, Remarque packed up his many art works—including paintings by Cézanne, Daumier, Degas, Delacroix, Picasso, Toulouse-Lautrec, Utrillo, and Van Gogh—in addition to a large collection of sculptures, Oriental rugs, antiques, and other art objects, while a frantic Jutta phoned him from Monte Carlo pleading to join him. Remarque responded that he had sent her money and advised her to get to Biarritz, a place close to the border with neutral Spain. By the end of October, Jutta arrived in New York and was detained on Ellis Island as her U.S. visa was found to be invalid. Remarque, who felt guilty for having abandoned her in Europe, immediately phoned immigration lawyers who arranged to have her deported to Mexico. His celebrity status surely helped to expedite the arrangements. Back in Hollywood, Remarque found himself surrounded by many other exiles involved in the activities of the Anti-Nazi League and the Joint Anti-Fascist Refugee Committee. Remarque, however, systematically avoided any political affiliation. In 1940 he traveled to Mexico City to see Jutta, and the two then legally entered the United States at the Tijuana border. In October 1941 Remarque applied for U.S. citizenship for which there was a five-year statutory waiting period. In 1942 Remarque returned to New York, his favorite city. In August of that year, he learned of the destruction of his home town of Osnabrück.

In the fall of 1943, Remarque's paintings and art works were exhibited at the prestigious Knoedler Gallery in New York. Amid the backdrop of war, the end of the year was further marred by personal tragedy for Remarque. On December 16 his sister, Elfriede Remark Scholz, having been denounced by two women whom she regarded as friends, was branded an "enemy of the state" and executed by the Nazis. In passing judgment, Judge Roland Friesler allegedly stated the following: "We have sentenced you to death because we cannot apprehend you brother. You must suffer for your brother." The effect on Remarque was one of profound shock, as well as guilt for having avoided any public statements about the grim circumstances in Europe. In response to her execution, Remarque began writing *Spark of Life*, set in a Nazi concentration camp, as a tribute to his sister.

In 1944 Remarque was working on *Arch of Triumph*, a novel in which the brutality of the Nazis is unequivocally embodied in the brutal character of Gestapo agent Haake. In the same year, the American Office of Strategic Services asked Remarque to assist them in writing "denazifying" propaganda, and he subsequently began working on *Practical Educational Work in Germany after the War*. *Arch of Triumph* was published in late 1945 and was a great success. Following hearings on his personal and political activities, Remarque became a naturalized U.S. citizen in August 1947, followed by his return to Switzerland in 1948 with the intention of traveling back and forth between the two countries. In late October, he met Jutta in Paris, returning to New York amid the growing concern of Remarque's failing health. He was soon diagnosed with

Ménière's disease, caused by excessive fluid in the labyrinth of the ears, a condition that could lead to deafness and vertigo.

While in New York, Remarque ran into the Hollywood star, Paulette Goddard, while walking along Fifth Avenue in April 1951, and the two soon entered the gossip columns as they dined in fashionable New York restaurants. Their relationship would prove to be a very happy one. Remarque, who had by then become a patient of the famous psychoanalyst, Karen Horney, had worked through many of his emotional issues and was receptive to Paulette's easygoing and carefree attitude toward life.

In 1952 *Spark of Life*, dedicated to P.G. (Paulette Goddard), was published in both English and German. While it became a *New York Times* best-seller, its German language edition, contracted to be published by the largest Swiss house, ran into unforeseeable trouble when that firm refused to print it on the grounds that it would be boycotted in Germany. Indeed, when the book was finally published by the Cologne firm of Kiepenheuer & Witsch in July 1952, it aroused hostile criticism from large sections of the population, though some accepted it without objection. Remarque's father died in 1954 leaving Erich with many regrets for having neglected him. That same year, *A Time to Love and a Time to Die* was published in both German and English. While the book was appreciated in America and Great Britain, it was not as warmly received in Germany, for it implicitly assigned culpability to the German people for being complicit with the Nazis. Many Germans were also angry at Remarque for living a life of ease far from the realities of existence under the Third Reich and consequently felt that he was not in a position to point the accusing finger. In August 1955 G.W. Pabst's film about Hitler's last days, *The Last Act*, for which Remarque wrote the scenario, premiered in Berlin and was shown at the Edinburgh Film Festival. In 1956 *The Black Obelisk* was published in German, and the play *The Last Station* premiered in Berlin in September. While living in Hollywood, Remarque wrote and consulted on Universal Studio's adaptation of *A Time to Love and a Time to Die* and in May 1957 he divorced Jutta once again, by mutual agreement, in Mexico. In February 1958 Remarque married Paulette Goddard, a woman twelve years his junior.

On November 1, 1964, Remarque received the Justus Möser Medal from the city of Osnabrück for distinguished and honored service, and in 1967 he was honored by the West German government with *Das Gross Verdienskreuz*, the distinguished service cross of the Order of Merit. These two honors were followed by distinguished literary recognition in West Germany and Remarque's election to the Deutsch Akademie für Sprache und Dichtung. In the midst of these tributes, Remarque suffered a second stroke in January 1965, though he recovered sufficiently to travel back to New York in the summer of 1966, a trip that had a salutary effect on his spirits. In autumn 1967 Remarque suffered two more strokes and was back in Porto Ronco to celebrate his seventieth birthday. In August 1970 he suffered his sixth and final stroke. He died on September 25, 1970, in Sant'Agathe Clinic in Locarno, Switzerland, and was buried in the cemetery, a short walk from the Casa Remarque.

In 1971 *Shadows in Paradise*, his novel portraying the lives of German exiles in New York City during World War II, was published posthumously.

The Story Behind the Story

When Remarque first submitted *All Quiet on the Western Front* for publication in spring 1928, he sent it to his employer Scherl Verlag, knowing in advance that the nationalistic sympathies of the company's owner, Hugenberg, would result in a rejection. His motivation to submit the manuscript nonetheless may have been simply a professional courtesy. A few months later, Remarque then sent his manuscript to Samuel Fischer Verlag, a leading German publisher, because Ullstein had done an unsatisfactory job of promoting his earlier novel, *Station on the Horizon*. S. Fischer Verlag had an impressive history having previously published such authors as Henrik Ibsen, Thomas Mann, Hermann Hesse, and Hugo von Hofmannsthal. Unfortunately and much to their disadvantage, however, Fischer Verlag did not think there was any interest in stories of World War I, especially ten years after its conclusion. Following their rejection, Remarque submitted his manuscript to Fritz Ross at the Ullstein publishing firm. Originally a publisher of newspapers and magazines, Ullstein had become quite successful in the 1920s. When Ross recommended *All Quiet* to his superior, Paul Wiegler, the decision was made to accept it, on the condition that the novel be initially published in serial form in Ullstein's liberal newspaper, the *Vossische Zeitung*. Ullstein also launched an unprecedented advertising campaign in its efforts to promote the novel and its author. One Remarque scholar, Angelika Howind of the Erich-Maria-Remarque Archiv in Osnabrück, has noted that the effect of Ullstein's clever sales strategy was to present a misleading characterization of the author and his motivation for writing the novel.

. . . [T]hey used all their tricks of advanced marketing to overcome the strong German militaristic tendencies. . . . They created an artificial EMR intending to separate his book from other war novels. By falsifying the data, they created the illusion that *All Quiet* was an autobiographical document written by an inexperienced, untutored representative of all front-line soldiers. They wrote that the diary was a catharsis.

The contentions of the advertisements clearly belied the biographical facts of Remarque's life, namely that he was an educated and experienced writer before he began the novel, that the circumstances of his military life were not nearly as dramatic as those faced by his protagonist Paul Bäumer and, further, that his book underwent a series of revisions before being submitted for publication. Most significantly, in a year in which the market was glutted with works on World War I, Ullstein was determined that *All Quiet* should be catapulted to fame and head the list of war stories during a period in 1929 and 1930 that became known as the "war boom."

Following the successful serialization plan, in which the *Vossiche Zeitung* was sold out each day, *All Quiet on the Western Front* then appeared in book form on January 29, 1929. Within three weeks, it sold 200,000 copies, followed by a large number of foreign language translations, twenty in total, including Chinese and Esperanto, as well as a German Braille copy which Ullstein also issued. In Great Britain, the Barrow public library had received two years' worth of advance reservations. The executives at Ullstein were so pleased with the book's success that they rewarded Remarque with his dream car, a pearl-gray Lancia, an undeniable status symbol the author embraced and went so far as to name "Puma." Remarque would have several accidents with his beloved car, the first in summer 1931, while at the fashionable Dutch resort of Noordwijk.

Notwithstanding *All Quiet*'s immediate and enormous success, it was nevertheless 1929, and the government of the Weimar Republic would soon exhibit signs of weakness and impending collapse. The publication of *All Quiet* occurred during a period of relative stability in Germany, mostly economically, a time known as Stresemann's Golden Era, where Gustav Stresemann served as foreign minister from 1923 to 1929. His death in 1929, at age fifty-one and four years after having received the Nobel Peace Prize, marked the beginning of the end of Stresemann's achievements. On March 29, 1930, the first Nazi official, Heinrich Brüning, was appointed finance minister. The same year, the Reichstag general elections, held on September 14, resulted in a radical political change, with the Nazis gaining an increased legislative presence to the detriment of the previous moderate majority. As a result of this rapidly changing political climate, *All Quiet on the Western Front* would become a victim of the Third Reich, for such a pacifist work was branded anathema to the German soldiers of World War I and an affront to German nationalism.

When the film version of *All Quiet* premiered in Berlin on December 4, 1930, Nazi hooligans reacted by staging a disgraceful protest. Joseph Goebbels, who was then head of the Nazi party in Berlin and supervisor of the Brown Shirts, ordered his men to attend the first showing and, with the lights dimmed, to unleash a pack of white mice and stink bombs, while hurling beer bottles and shouting at the audience. Though the theater's manager tried to capture the mice and some of the audience remained, the screening was canceled that evening and, later on, forbidden. A few years after this incident, in spring 1932, the German government seized Remarque's account at the Darmstadt and National Bank in Berlin, though he remained a German citizen while traveling back and forth from Switzerland. Finally, in the early morning hours of January 29, 1933, just hours away from Hitler becoming Germany's chancellor, Remarque left on the advice of a friend, taking his dog, Billy, and drove to Switzerland with only the clothes on his back. On the evening of May 10, 1933, Joseph Goebbels launched a massive public burning of books, some 20,000 in number, deemed necessary as a cleansing of "degenerate" art. *All Quiet on the Western Front* was considered one of these immoral works. Later, in November 1933, an additional 3,411 copies were seized from the Ullstein publishing house as "protection for the German people." A few weeks later, on December 4, those copies were destroyed by the Gestapo. Erich Maria Remarque would learn of these events from a radio broadcast, while drinking Rhine wine in Switzerland with another writer in exile, Emil Ludwig.

List of Characters

Paul Bäumer is both the narrator and protagonist of *All Quiet on the Western Front*. Like his comrades, he is a young German soldier who has volunteered for military duty during World War I on the advice and encouragement of his teacher. During the course of his experiences, Bäumer forms a profound bond with his friends. As he loses them one by one in a never-ending series of catastrophes, Bäumer grows more depressed by and disillusioned with the war. The last of the young soldiers to have survived, he is killed just ahead of the armistice on a day in which all was quiet on the front.

Kantorek is a teacher at the school that Bäumer and his friends attended. Small in stature, he is nonetheless an influential and misguided authority figure who glorifies war and sacrifice for the German fatherland. His students become bitter and resentful for having encouraged them to join the military and later hold him responsible for the death of Josef Behm, the first of the classmates to be killed in the war.

Stanislaus Katczinsky is a shrewd forty-year-old soldier who becomes Bäumer's best friend. Nicknamed Kat, he is good natured and resourceful, always managing to find extra food and supplies and easy jobs for Bäumer's group of friends. His death near the end of the novel is a terrible blow to Bäumer.

Muller is a fellow soldier and one of Bäumer's classmates. Muller misses his school days and often carries his books with him. He is also an example of the pragmatic thinking that is necessary for survival, when he asks Kemmerich for his yellow leather boots since the fellow soldier has had one of his legs amputated.

Albert Kropp is another soldier and one of Bäumer's classmates. As a creative thinker, Kropp comes up with the idea of putting the generals from both sides of the war into an arena where they can slug it out for themselves. A close companion of Paul Bäumer while they lie in a hospital, Kropp's leg is amputated, after which he is sent to an institute to be fitted for an artificial limb.

Tjaden is a "skinny lock-smith" who has a voracious appetite, though Bäumer cannot figure out where he puts all his food. Tjaden exhibits intelligence as the soldiers remonstrate on who exactly is responsible for the war.

Franz Kemmerich is a childhood friend of Bäumer and student of Kantorek who also joins the military. When he dies early in the narrative after his leg is amputated, his coveted yellow leather boots are given to Muller.

Josef Behm is the first of Bäumer's classmates to enlist in the army and the first to be killed in the war. His classmates hold Kantorek responsible for his death.

Leer is another of Bäumer's classmates who joins the infantry at Kantorek's misguided encouragement. Somewhat a rebel, he grows a beard and has relationships with women.

Corporal Himmelstoss is a sadistic drillmaster who enjoys tormenting the soldiers. A postman before joining the army, he uses his new position to bully others until he is taught a painful lesson and later shamed into putting on a brave front after Bäumer discovers him cowering in a trench.

Gérard Duval is the French soldier who falls into Bäumer's shell hole and is stabbed by him in a moment of panic. Bäumer is soon filled with remorse for what he has done and attempts to bandage Duval's wounds. This tragic incident will cause Bäumer to understand that the enemy is just another frightened soldier like him.

Haie Westhus is one of the soldiers in Bäumer's infantry unit. After the war is over, he wants to stay in the peace-time army, preferring the military to a civilian life digging peat. However, he does not survive the war.

Detering is a soldier in Bäumer's unit who is forever dreaming of his farm and family. One day, when he sees a blossoming cherry tree, his desire to return home gets the best of him, and he deserts the infantry. Detering is soon arrested and then heard from no more.

Lieutenant Bertnick is the company commander, respected by Bäumer and his friends for his bravery and heroic deeds in trying to defend them.

Ginger is the company cook who closely guards the food from the hungry soldiers. He is an example of someone who blindly and unquestioningly follows orders without thinking about his actions.

Summary and Analysis

Chapter 1 begins with a group of German soldiers on the western front, having endured fourteen days of intense fighting. We are introduced to the protagonist, Paul Bäumer, as he observes his comrades, Tjaden and Muller, eating as much as they possibly can. Bäumer wonders where the emaciated Tjaden, "who is thin as a grasshopper," puts all this food. Paul Bäumer will narrate nearly the entire horrific story of what these young school friends experience during their military service. Only nineteen years of age, Bäumer has enlisted as a result of the misguided advice he received from his high school teacher, Kantorek, who went so far as to glorify the war for his students and encourage them to do their patriotic duty in defending the German homeland. His other classmates—Kropp, Behm, and Leer—also join him at the front, because they, too, are the recipients of the same bad counsel. These young men are comrades in arms along with Tjaden, Westhus, Detering, and Katczinsky.

It is about noontime, and the unit is eagerly awaiting a hearty meal from the soup kitchen. The cook, Ginger, has prepared a meal for 150 men, although the company has now been reduced to eighty since so many soldiers did not survive the battle. The cook, however, an example of blind and unquestioning obedience to orders, states that he can only distribute food for eighty soldiers. The soldiers argue with him and eventually prevail. Following lunch, the mail is distributed, and we learn that Kantorek, the young soldiers' former schoolmaster, "an active little man in a grey tail-coat, with a face like a shrew-mouse," has written a letter. A discussion ensues in which the former schoolmates recall how radically different their attitude has become regarding their former teacher. While in school, they idolized Kantorek, but that admiration has now changed to hate as they hold him responsible for their present suffering and for depriving them of their youth. As Bäumer states, "While they continued to write and talk, we saw the wounded and dying. While they taught that duty to one's country is the greatest thing, we already knew that death-throes are stronger." The enlisted men believe that Kantorek's culpability goes even further, as they hold him responsible for the death of Josef Behm, the first of them to be killed when Bäumer's company was unable to rescue him because they were themselves under attack. Beyond their animosity to Kantorek is an even larger truth, namely that these young soldiers, who have tasted the bitterness of war, have come to hate all institutions and forms of authority. "The first bombardment showed us our mistake, and under it the world as they had taught it to us broke in pieces." These young men have lost all confidence in a foreseeable future and their spirits continue to sink lower.

Franz Kemmerich then becomes the focus of the narrative, and we are presented with the shocking details of his irreparable wounds. Kemmerich, who is lying in a makeshift hospital, "that reeks as ever of carbolic, ether, and sweat," has just had his leg amputated. "His features have become uncertain and faint, like a photographic plate on which two pictures have been taken." To make matters worse, there is very little morphine available, and it seems that Kemmerich is destined not to receive any, until Bäumer and his friends bribe an apathetic orderly into administering the medication. For his part, despite his dire situation, Kemmerich is worried that his watch has been stolen by someone at the hospital. While Bäumer and the others try to console Kemmerich, Muller is busy eyeing Kemmerich's prized yellow leather boots and tries to persuade Kemmerich to give them up, for Muller knows that even if Kemmerich lives, he no longer has a need for two boots. The grim reality underlying the request is that if Muller does not take them, some dishonest hospital worker surely will.

As Bäumer reflects back on his past life as a student (**Chapter 2**), he thinks of former days when he had time to write poetry, a carefree period that has regrettably passed away. "Many an evening I have worked over them—we all did something of the kind—but that has become so unreal to me that I cannot comprehend it any more." Thinking about home, Bäumer now sees how the youth of all soldiers is foreshortened and that this change can only be understood in retrospect, for while they were still in school they were too young to comprehend fully what it meant to go war. Bäumer's reflections universalize the realities and horrors faced by young soldiers at war, not just specifically during World War I, but in all conflicts. Though *All Quiet* specifically relates to World War I, one of Remarque's achievements is to show how his message has a far-reaching relevance to all people. After ten weeks on the front, the soldiers feel bereft of meaningful human relationships and any opportunity to enjoy life. "We know only that in some strange and melancholy way we have become a waste land."

As Bäumer's thoughts turn to Muller's unfeeling attitude toward Kemmerich's imminent death, thinking only about how well Kemmerich's boots would fit him, Bäumer concludes that Muller is simply being practical rather than deeply insensitive. "He merely sees things clearly." From Bäumer's perspective, Muller is acting on the premise that each soldier must ensure his own survival, for the harsh reality of war does not allow for sentimentality or unexpected charity. "We have lost all sense of other considerations, because they are artificial. Only the facts are real and important to us. And good boots are scarce." As Bäumer sees it, ten weeks of training in the army has had a far greater impact than his ten years of schooling: "We learned that a bright button is weightier than four volumes of Schopenhauer."

As part of his musings on the grim details of war, Bäumer thinks about his drillmaster's cruelty. Corporal Himmelstoss is a bully and a sadist, and Bäumer gives numerous examples of his vicious character. "Together with Kropp, Westhus, and Tjaden I have stood at attention in a hard frost without gloves for a quarter of an hour at a stretch, while Himmelstoss watched for the slightest movements of our bare fingers on the steel barrel of a rifle." Despite his pervasive cruelty, Himmelstoss never succeeds on an emotional level, as the group remains defiant and Bäumer relates the particular moment when he and his friends had had enough abuse. "We obeyed each order. . . . But we did it so slowly that Himmelstoss became desperate. . . . But before we had even begun to sweat, he was hoarse. After that he left us in peace." While standing up to this abusive corporal was essential to their survival, Bäumer is also relaying another important message that runs throughout *All Quiet*, a positive celebration of the camaraderie that is fostered by the harsh conditions of war, "a practical esprit de corps."

As Bäumer turns his thoughts again to Kemmerich, his cherished childhood friend, and his last moments before death, he remembers how heartrending it was to listen to Kemmerich's brave words when facing his amputation. "What is it anyway—an amputated leg? here they patch up far worse things than that." Still, the most poignant recollection of all is Kemmerich's regret that he will never be able to fulfill his dream of becoming a head forester. Though he listens to Bäumer's consolatory advice that there are "splendid artificial limbs," he has no response, and his silence is both powerful and emotionally charged. Instead, in a tacit acknowledgment that his life is over, he tells Bäumer that Muller can have his boots. In agonizing detail, Bäumer recounts the minute details of Kemmerich's demise. "An hour passes. I sit tensely and watch his every movement in case he may perhaps say something. . . . But he only weeps, his head turned aside." And, with Kemmerich's death just moments away, Bäumer remembers his attempts to find a doctor to help and, sadly, how the doctor refused. The doctor's response is that he cannot possibly remember Kemmerich since he has already performed five amputations that day as he hurries off to the operating room to perform yet another, the business of amputation taking on a factorylike quality with so many being done each day. By the time Bäumer gets back to Kemmerich, the young man is dead. In a scene devoid of any sensitivity to the precariousness of human life, Kemmerich is immediately removed from the bed so as to make space for another patient, as the orderly asks whether Bäumer will be taking his things. Once outside the hospital, Bäumer thinks about how lucky he is to be alive. "Thoughts of girls, of flowery meadows, of white clouds suddenly come into my head."

Chapter 3 opens with Paul Bäumer and his friends adopting a superior attitude as new and inexperienced recruits arrive on the scene. "We stick out our chests, shave in the open, shove our hands in our pockets, inspect the recruits and feel ourselves to be stone-age veterans." Katczinsky advises one of the novices that his allotment of bread with turnips is far preferable to being served sawdust for a meal. For his part, Kat, always resourceful in the sparsest of situations, manages to procure beef stew and string beans for himself as he explains how he accomplished this feat. "Ginger was glad I took it. I gave him three pieces of parachute silk for it." Bäumer also says that Katczinsky is particularly adept in sensing where to find those things necessary for survival in the most desolate places. "We stir a bit as the door opens and Kat appears. I think I must be dreaming; he has two loaves of bread under his arm and a blood-stained sandbag full of horse-flesh in his hand."

As they sit in their hut, Tjaden, who neglected to salute a major, is of the opinion that the war is already lost because they salute so well, a comment that provokes Katczinsky. While the two argue, an air battle is being waged above them. Kat observes that if all soldiers were treated equally, with everyone receiving same compensation and food rations, the war between Germany and the Allies would be over, for their leaders would have no incentive to keep the war going. "Give 'em all the same grub and all the same pay / And the war would be over and done in a day." Once again, we are reminded of the class distinctions within the army and the inequities that result. In response, Kropp proposes another hypothetical condition, namely that if the ministers and generals of both countries were to be armed with clubs and sent into an arena to fight it out, the war would also end quickly, as the survivor would simply be declared the victor. Kropp further observes another grim fact he has learned about human nature in war as he notes that the more an individual feels marginalized in civilian life, the more likely he is to treat others inhumanely when he becomes an officer in the army, echoing similar sentiments previously expressed and marking one of the novel's themes. "As sure as they get a stripe or a star they become different men, just as though they'd swallowed concrete." An example of this contention is readily at hand in Himmelstoss who, prior to the war, was a simple mailman who has since become drunk with power. Katczinsky goes on to observe that military life brings on a terrible transformation in men: "In himself man is essentially a beast, only he butters it over like a slice of bread with a little decorum. The army is based on that. . . ." As Himmelstoss arrives, the young men recall how they got their revenge. One dark night, they trapped Himmelstoss by placing a blanket over his head, and then proceeded to beat him. Since Himmelstoss was never able to identify them, they got away without suffering any consequences and were celebrated as heroes by the other soldiers in their camp. "That evening's work made us more or less content to leave next morning. And an old buffer was pleased to describe us as 'young heroes.'"

Chapter 4 opens with a perilous situation as Bäumer's unit is put in charge of placing barbed wire along parts of the frontline. The young soldiers reach their destination in the dark, with the odor of dense smoke and the sound of artillery explosions all around. Along the way, Bäumer hears the sound of geese, "aspirants for the frying-pan," and Katczinsky makes note of it as well, stating that he intends to come back for them when the moment is right. Though Bäumer and his "veteran" soldiers are not afraid, the story is quite different for the new recruits. "It is not fear. Men who have been up as often as we have become thick-skinned. Only the young recruits are agitated." All the same, Baumer continues to portray the landscape of the front, and the soldiers' response to it, as he describes the comfort and protection to be found in the earth beneath their feet. "To no man does the earth mean so much as to the soldier. . . . [H]e stifles his terror and his cries in her silence and her security; she shelters him and gives him a new lease of ten seconds of life, receives him again and often for ever." As Bäumer astutely points out, the earth is primeval and the human response to it is likewise primitive and instinctive. "By the animal instinct that is awakened in us we are led and protected. It is not conscious; it is far quicker, much more sure, less fallible than consciousness."

As Bäumer continues to describe the terrain from his vantage point in the woods, it is from a highly depersonalized perspective. Difficult to discern precise details in the pervasive smoke and fog, he creates an image of his surroundings that echoes the universal theme of the loss of individuality and humanity that takes place among military recruits, reduced to the status of objects. "Here the heads become figures; coats, trousers, and boots appear out of the mist. . . . [I]ndividuals are no longer recognizable, the dark wedge presses onward. . . ." Adding to the misery are the anguished sounds of wounded horses, which in turn symbolize the suffering that mankind has created through war, namely empty sacrifice. "It is the moaning of the world, it is the martyred creation, wild with anguish, filled with terror, and groaning." Detering, a farmer by occupation, is so distraught by the horses' agony that he cries out to shoot them as an act of mercy, but the wounded men must be attended to first. Eventually, though, the horses are shot.

At three o'clock in the morning, the shelling resumes, and the only viable cover for the soldiers is the graveyard. Bäumer is bombarded with splinters and shrapnel, though he is not seriously wounded. As he manages to crawl to safety in a hole, he finds himself side by side with a coffin and a corpse. "I open my eyes—my fingers grasp a sleeve, an arm. My hand gropes further, splinters of wood—now I remember that we are lying in the graveyard." These horrors notwithstanding, Bäumer is compelled to stay where he is because a gas attack has been initiated. As the attack continues, more soldiers are killed or injured and more dead bodies are thrown out of their coffins and deposited into the graveyard. "With a crash, something black bears down on us. It lands close beside us; a coffin thrown open."

Once the shelling stops and the men are able to take off their masks, they discover that one of the new recruits, with whom Kat had previously joked, has been fatally injured and is close to death. "He is the fair-haired boy of a little while ago." Bäumer and Kat consider whether they should shoot the young man as an act of mercy—for his pain is intense and he will soon die—but the remainder of the unit arrives during their moment of deliberation, and the young man is instead carried off on a stretcher. "Every day that he can live will be a howling torture."

As the soldiers return to their huts (**Chapter 5**), they occupy their time killing lice, while trying to imagine what they will do if the war ends and they return to civilian life. The responses vary; while Kat is realistic and wants to get home to take care of his family, Bäumer points out that Kat has a wife and children, something the others lack. Haie Westhus eventually admits that he "would stay with the Prussians and serve out [his] time." Once again, we are reminded of how the soldiers' youth has been irrevocably squandered by war and has left them with little hope. At the moment, they are awaiting Himmelstoss, who has reportedly "overdone it with a couple of young recruits," so as to enact revenge on him. Tjaden's dreams of the future are narrowly focused, as he is immersed in the thought of devoting the rest of his life to Himmelstoss's torture. When asked what he would do should the war end, Tjaden states: "'See to it that Himmelstoss doesn't get past me.' Apparently he would like most to have him in a cage and sail into him with a club every morning." Bäumer, however, is the one who best expresses their despair, for their young lives have been destroyed just as their hope for the future has been compromised. "We were eighteen and had begun to love life and the world; and we had to shoot it to pieces. . . . We are cut off from activity, from striving, from progress."

When Himmelstoss arrives, he clearly expects the young men to stand up and show him the respect he believes they are obligated to show a superior office. When no one budges, Himmelstoss is at a loss. "He has no idea what to make of the situation. He didn't expect this open hostility." Tjaden is the first to respond verbally, in the form of an insult. In response to Himmelstoss's sarcastic question whether the two met in the gutter, Tjaden quickly tosses the abusive comment back to Himmelstoss. "'No, you slept there by yourself.'" Needless to say, Himmelstoss, "a raging book of army regulations," is infuriated and storms out threatening punitive action. The group then resumes discussing what they will do when the war ends, and the conversation turns to the merits of the education they received from Kantorek, as opposed to the practical one they received from the army. Once again, the soldiers note how those who were too young to have started their lives before the war now lack the ability to return to a normal life, because they never had the opportunity to grow up first. "We are cut off from activity, from striving, from progress. We believe in such things no longer, we believe in the war."

Eventually, the company commander, Lieutenant Bertinck, becomes involved in Himmelstoss's charge that the young men were insubordinate. The case goes to trial, which takes place in the orderly room with Bäumer being called as a witness to explain Tjaden's behavior. Though Bertinck is sympathetic to the young men, demanding an admission of guilt from Himmelstoss for his punishment of bed wetting, he is compelled to mete out punishment for the soldiers' insubordination. The reprimand is nonetheless light with Tjaden and Kropp receiving "open arrest." "An hour after Tjaden and Kropp are settled in behind their wire-netting we make our way in to them. . . . Tjaden greets us crowing. . . . Tjaden wins of course, the lucky wretch." **Chapter 5** concludes with Bäumer and Kat roasting a goose they stole from a shed belonging to regimental headquarters where Bäumer was forced to contend with a threatening bulldog, ultimately managing to escape. For a brief moment in time, as they share their meal, there is a glimmer of happiness amid the death and destruction with which they are surrounded. "We are brothers and press on one another the choicest pieces."

Chapter 6 begins with a conversation amongst the soldiers that can best be described as gallows humor. As they look at the more than one hundred coffins stacked against a wall and realize this is done in anticipation of the first night of the offensive, they express their anxiety by joking about it. "'You be thankful if you get so much as a coffin,' grins Tjaden, 'they'll slip you a waterproof sheet for your old Aunt Sally of a carcass.'" The humor at the front is as grim as their circumstances. The chapter introduces two metaphors to express the continuing downward spiral of the soldiers' morale and behavior in the face of daily deprivation and their struggle to stay alive in a world where time is reckoned in moments rather than days.

The first is the comparison between the lives of the soldiers to that of animals who are driven simply by the survival instinct, an urge that motivates violence and killing in the face of an unrelenting assault by the enemy and a scarcity of food and water necessary to maintain that minimal existence. We are introduced to the animal analogy when Bäumer describes their mode of existence as comparable to living in a cage where they wait in fear for whatever may befall them. "We lie under the network of arching shells and live in a suspense of uncertainty." The most horrible image of the trenches, however, is Bäumer's description of the thousands of trench rats they must fight off. "They have shocking, evil, naked faces, and it is nauseating to see their long, nude tails." Adding to this nightmare is the fact that they are forced to compete with these vermin, who "seem to be mighty hungry" for every morsel of food, as they gnaw the soldiers bread. The soldiers are compelled to devise a means to outwit these voracious scavengers. "The slices we cut off are heaped together in the middle of the floor. Each man takes out his spade and lies down prepared to strike." Ironically, when food does arrive in the form of rations of Edamer cheese, it is interpreted as an ominous sign because "the fat red balls have long been a sign of a bad time coming."

As the bombardment continues relentlessly, Bäumer's trench is almost entirely destroyed. When the company commander arrives and announces that an effort will be made to bring in food, everyone is relieved. However, there are certainly no guarantees this will be possible and, after two attempts to deliver rations, the party bringing the food must turn back. Even the ever-resourceful Kat fails in his efforts and the men are left with their own unnegotiable hunger. "We pull in our belts tighter and chew every mouthful three times as long." Their hunger grows so intense that Tjaden bemoans the fact that in an effort to chase the rats away, they gave up the gnawed parts of the bread.

Throughout this ordeal, Bäumer reports that the recruits are the most vulnerable and least able to cope with the chaos that surrounds them. "One of the recruits has a fit. . . . These hunted, protruding eyes, we know them too well. During the last few hours he has had merely the appearance of a clam. He had collapsed like a rotten tree." With this scene and the intervention by Kat and Bäumer, who must restrain the recruit from leaving the dugout, we are once again reminded of the theme of innocent youth unprepared to face the nightmare into which it is thrown.

After a difficult time with several other recruits who appear to be succumbing to the pressures of the battlefront, Kat proposes a game of skat, a German card game from the early 1800s, but to no avail, for they are distracted with every explosion going on around them and instead become paralyzed by the relentless strain and the apprehension about what the next moment holds. "We have neither flesh nor muscles any longer, we dare not look at one another for fear of some incalculable thing. So we shut our teeth—it will end—it will end—perhaps we will come through." The explosions eventually stop and, when they do, the brief silence signals an oncoming attack. A nightmarish scene ensues in which several soldiers have their skulls blown open, while others have been dismembered. Bäumer describes a brief instance in which he looks into the eyes of a Frenchman and stops in his tracks for a moment before throwing a grenade right at him. "I raise my hand but I cannot throw into those strange eyes; for one mad moment the whole slaughter whirls like a circus round me. . . ." Nevertheless, each moment is a struggle to survive and a mandate to kill the enemy before he kills you. "We have become wild beasts. We do not fight, we defend ourselves against annihilation."

As the soldiers become embroiled in a fight for their lives, Bäumer vows that if the situation were such and his father had been fighting with the Allies, he would kill him. "If your own father came over with them you would not hesitate to fling a bomb into them." The following afternoon, as the German counterattack shows signs of success and Bäumer and his company find a more suitable trench, he reflects on the never-ending pattern of crawling into a shelter and climbing out again. In this new setting, a second metaphoric image emerges to embody the inhumanity of life at the front. "We reach the shelter of the reserves and yearn to creep in and disappear;—but instead we must turn round and plunge again into the horror." Bäumer observes that this unstoppable pattern of retreat and return has transformed the men into machines, a state in which action is privileged over thought, an instinctive mode of behavior necessary to their survival but all the same containing the inhumane qualities the analogy implies. "If we were not automata at that moment we would continue lying there, exhausted, and without will. But we are swept forward again, powerless, madly savage and raging; we will kill, for they are still our mortal enemies. . . ." For Bäumer, the war has brought about a terrible change in them,"[w]e have lost all feeling for one another," though this situation does not apply to the unshakeable camaraderie shared by his small circle of friends. Rather, Bäumer refers in general to the lack of sensitivity to the enemy forces, soldiers who are in fact young men like them and with whom in reality they have no quarrel.

As time passes, Bäumer begins to reminisce about home as he remembers the enticing quietness and appealing coolness of the cathedral cloister, an escape from the horrific sights and sounds of death. At the same time, this fond memory also provokes a question about his future and the youth that has all but passed him by while at the front. "A great quietness rules in this blossoming quadrangle. . . . I stand there and wonder whether, when I am twenty, I shall have experienced the bewildering emotions of love." Ultimately, the alluring stillness of these images is a cause for alarm as the haunting realization begins to grip him, namely that they are recollections of a previous and highly desirable life to which he may not return. "They are soundless apparitions that speak to me . . . and it is the alarm of their silence that forces me to lay hold of my sleeve and my rifle lest I should abandon myself to the liberation and allurement in which my body would dilate and gently pass away into the still forces that lie behind these things." These pleasing memories of former joy and happiness become a source of great pain, as Bäumer believes them eminently unattainable. At the same time, he understands that he has been irrevocably changed by his nightmare existence on the front. "We could never again, as the same beings, take part in those scenes."

Little changes for the men, the same dangerous monotony of attacks and counterattacks being the one predictable and consistent aspect of their lives. Bäumer relates how some of the wounded are far from their reach and must wait hours for rescue, often dying in the interim, while those in the trenches must listen to their last hours of agony. As they search in vain for two days for one of their company, they can detect his voice but find him nowhere, especially since they cannot perceive any movement. "On the second day the calls are fainter; that will be because his lips and mouth have become dry."

At night, Bäumer and some of his friends search for "copper driving-bands and the silken parachutes of the French star-shells." Though Bäumer does not understand how or why the driving bands might be useful, Haie Westhus explains that his girlfriend will use them to supplement her garters, while Tjaden enjoys putting his legs through the largest of the rings. The soldiers muse that the silk parachutes could be sent home to the women to make clothing, though Bäumer and Kropp use them as handkerchiefs.

As trench warfare persists throughout the summer, with the same plagues and complaints as always, Bäumer's discussion turns once again to the vulnerability of the recruits who arrive at the front with no understanding of the perils they face and no experience in how best to maneuver. From Bäumer's description, their function at the front is a purely sacrificial one. "They are helpless in this grim fighting area, they fall like flies. The present method of fighting from posts demands knowledge and experience. . . ," which they tragically lack. Once again, we are reminded of the heartbreaking loss of young lives robbed of their youth and the ability to realize their as yet unfulfilled promise. Instead, the soldiers' lives are choked off, in some instances literally, when subject to a surprise gas attack. "They have not yet learned what to do."

Himmelstoss then reenters the narrative, this time discovered in a trench "with a small scratch lying in a corner pretending to be wounded. Bäumer is enraged when he finds him thus, refusing to move, and proceeds to force him out of his shelter. "I grab him by the neck and shake him like a sack, his head jerks from side to side." Himmelstoss leaves his display of cowardice in the trench and, once outside, to no great surprise, he becomes a dutiful soldier obeying a lieutenant's orders. "Once more he is the smart Himmelstoss of the parade-ground, he has even outstripped the lieutenant and is far ahead."

The bombardment resumes, as does the horror it brings. Bäumer notes how weary the men are and how they have lost all track of time. Time exists only in days and in the relentless cycle of struggling to stay alive for one more. Yet, for all their suffering, those who have managed to stay alive are looked upon by the less fortunate as leading a charmed existence. "We see time pass in the colourless faces of the dying, we cram food into us, we run, we throw, we shoot, we kill, . . . still more helpless one there who, with staring eyes, look upon us as gods that escape death many times."

Having staved off the enemy for the moment, it is now autumn and time for Bäumer's company to be relieved, though only thirty-two men, from the original one hundred and fifty, remain. The company commander, calling out the names, has difficulty accepting this harsh reality, as he finally gives the marching order. "A line, a short line, trudges off into the morning. Thirty-two men."

Chapter 7 opens with a brief respite for Bäumer's unit, which has sustained major casualties. Those who have survived are taken to a field depot for rest. Within this encapsulated time and circumscribed context, the soldiers briefly forget the war. As Bäumer reports, even Himmelstoss, who shows up a few days later, appears to have been chastened by the war. "He has had the bounce knocked out of him since he has been in the trenches and wants to get on good terms with us." Bäumer is willing to acquiesce, primarily for Himmelstoss's caring for Westhus and his generosity with the soldiers at the canteen. Furthermore, Himmelstoss has now become the sergeant cook, a change of role that can work to the advantage of Bäumer's company. Bäumer is acutely aware, however, that the nightmares of battlefield mayhem will return. "And this I know: all these things that now, while we are still in the war, sink down in us like a stone, after the war shall waken again, and then shall begin the disentanglement of life and death." When Bäumer and his friends see a poster of an attractive woman, it revives memories of former happy times and reminds them that there is more to life than their grim existence at the front. This reminder of another altogether alternate existence, in turn, spurs them to find some sort of amusement, so they decide to go swimming in the canal. While they are enjoying the water, they make friends with three French women, who symbolize their engagement with the enemy, as France is a part of the Allied forces. While trying to make jokes and receiving incomprehensible answers in French from the women, Tjaden decides to entice them by producing a loaf of army bread. His action produces the desired effect and, despite the fact that both the soldiers and the girls are forbidden to cross to the opposite bank, the boys proceed to plan a nighttime rendezvous when they guards cannot see them. The girls agree and ask them to bring more bread. "Eagerly we assure them that we will bring some with us. And other tasty bits too, we roll our eyes and try to explain with our hands."

The gathering turns out to be fun, an experience opposite to the dreadful conditions they had been experiencing. "But then I feel the lips of the little brunette and press myself against them, my eyes close and I let it all fall from me, war and terror and grossness, in order to awaken young and happy. . . . And if I press deeper into the arms that embrace me, perhaps a miracle may happen. . . ." When they return to their barracks, Bäumer is granted seventeen days leave and decides to go home, a journey back to his previous life that will prove to be bittersweet. "The names of the stations begin to take on meaning and my heart trembles. . . . These names mark the boundaries of my youth." While on the train, the gentle landscape, marked with meadows and farms, can be seen through the window and are a radical change from the sights of the battlefield. When he arrives at his destination, Bäumer gives a detailed description of life in his hometown. "In this confectioner's we used to eat ices, and there we learned to smoke cigarettes. Walking down the street I know every shop, the colonial warehouses, the chemist's, the tobacconist's." Bäumer eventually reaches home where potato cakes are being prepared for his welcome. But things are nevertheless very different, and he is unsure how to respond to his sister who cries out with joy at seeing him. "I support myself with the butt of my rifle against my feet and clench my teeth fiercely, but I cannot speak a word, my sister's call has made me powerless, I can do nothing. . . ." Bäumer soon discovers that he can no longer connect to his family. "There is my mother, there is my sister, there my case of butterflies, and there the mahogany piano—but I am not myself there. There is a distance a veil between us." His family has always been poor but has endured its hardships without complaint. His wartime service has created an unbridgeable gap with both his family and his former life. As he sits with his mother, who is gravely ill, he is forced to minimize the dangers and deprivation he must endure at the front for her sake.

While Bäumer is headed to the district commandant to report his presence, he runs into a major and their exchange enrages him. Bäumer is upbraided for not properly addressing an officer and is forced into a marching exercise to appease the offended major. "I am mad with rage. But I cannot say anything to him; he could put me under arrest if he liked." When he returns home, he changes into civilian clothes, which displeases his father who would like to show off his soldier son in uniform. As the two sit in a local beer garden, Bäumer notes the alienation his recent experiences have engendered in him. "He wants me to tell him about the front; he is curious in a way that I find stupid and distressing; I no longer have any real contact with him. . . . What would become of us if everything that happens out there were quite clear to us?" Bäumer soon learns that his prior acquaintances are now irritating at best, as he meets his former German master who asks for news about the front and shows no understanding of the horrors the soldiers must endure. "I explain that no one would be sorry to be back home. He laughs uproariously. 'I can we believe it! But first you have to give the Froggies a good hiding.'" The acquaintance thinks that the daily activities of hometown life no longer interest Bäumer, while Bäumer feels resentful of the carefree spirit of his small community sheltered from the war. "When I see them here, in their rooms, in their offices, about their occupations, I feel an irresistible attraction in it, I would like to be here too and forget the war; but also it repels me, it is so narrow, . . .—They are different men here, men I cannot properly understand, whom I envy and despise." Likewise, the books that used to be meaningful to Bäumer no longer transport him to "the quick joy in the world of thought." Instead, he finds himself unable to even read. I stand there dumb. "As before a judge. Dejected. Words, Words, Words—they do not reach me. Slowly I place the books back in the shelves. Nevermore."

Bäumer then goes out to the barracks to meet with Mittelstadt who informs him that he has gotten his revenge on Kantorek who has been called up as a territorial who Mittelstadt has authority over now. It is another sequence of ironic developments that Kantorek has been assigned to the company of one of his former students, Commander Mittelstadt, who takes great satisfaction in tormenting his former teacher. Among other things, Mittelstadt holds Kantorek responsible for the death of Joseph Behm, who would not have enlisted if it were not for Kantorek's encouragement. Mittelstadt is offered the chance to teach his former teacher a lesson, as he subjects Kantorek to an array of disciplinary exercises, including absurd and exhausting marches.

Bäumer muses on the true definition of military leave, a painful experience that produces nothing positive: "A pause that only makes everything after it so much worse." Nevertheless, before he leaves, Bäumer visits Kemmerich's mother with the intention of bringing solace and comfort, and decides to lie to her in explaining that her son's death was immediate. Though she is angry and protests Bäumer's description, in the end she accepts his explanation. "As I leave she kisses me and gives me a picture of him."

Chapter 7 concludes with Bäumer even more psychologically fractured, as a result of his leave. He believes his time at home has made matters worse for him, for he now worries about his dying mother and mourns for all that his been fundamentally changed for him by his military service. "I was a soldier, and now I am nothing but an agony for myself, for my mother, for everything that is so comfortless and without end."

With his leave over, Bäumer is sent to a training camp near his hometown (**Chapter 8**). His days are occupied by a routine company drill, which he goes through "mechanically," while his evenings are spent in the Soldiers' Home where he has access to a piano. The ambiance of this relaxed setting exists in stark contrast to the war front, and for a brief moment, the fighting seems a distant reality. Bäumer's description of his time at the camp is reminiscent of a Romantic poet exulting in the beauty of his surroundings. "I often become so lost in the play of soft light and transparent shadow, that I almost fail to hear the commands. It is when one is alone that one begins to observe Nature and to love her." Bäumer, however, makes no attempt to find new friends.

Next door to the training camp, there is a Russian prisoner-of-war camp that affords Bäumer the opportunity to observe its inhabitants daily and realize that the enemy is made up of ordinary people. Bäumer describes them as "quiet people, men with their childlike faces and apostles' beards" and reflects on the arbitrariness by which a man becomes a sworn enemy. "Any non-commissioned officer is more of an enemy to a recruit, any schoolmaster to a pupil than they are to us." Bäumer stops himself when he remembers that such thoughts are dangerous at such a moment in time. "This way lies the abyss. It is not now the time; but I will not lose these thoughts, I will keep them away until the war is ended." Most of the prisoners, however, appear to be dying. "They are all rather feeble, for they only get enough nourishment to keep them from starving" and search for scraps of food in the garbage or sell their trinkets to the Germans in order to buy food. The items are traded at a loss, given the amount of labor the prisoners have expended in fashioning them. "But most of the Russians have long since parted with whatever things they had. Now they wear only the most pitiful clothing, and try to exchange little carvings and objects they have made out of shell fragments and copper bands." When Bäumer's family pays him an occasional visit, he can barely tolerate their brief time together. They tell him that his mother is in the hospital and will soon undergo an operation for her cancer. Their conversation is depressing and focused on their dire financial circumstances. This litany of gloom only prompts Bäumer's own bitter social commentary. "Yes, I think bitterly, that's how it is with us, and with all poor people. They don't dare to ask the price, but worry themselves dreadfully beforehand about it, but the others, for whom it is not important, they settle the price first as a matter of course." When they leave, Bäumer shares some of his food with the prisoners, while remembering the pains his mother took to cook it.

When Bäumer returns to his unit (**Chapter 9**), they travel for several days to an undisclosed destination where the fighting is the heaviest. He inquires after Kat and Albert, but to no avail. After a few days, he is told to report to the orderly room where a sergeant major questions him about his time on leave. Bäumer proceeds to bide his time, until he happily rejoins his company. For the moment, he feels rejuvenated and whole again as he shares his potato cakes and jam with his friends. However, his contentment will not last for long, as distant rumblings shake their hut.

Excitement grips the troops, with the announcement that the kaiser is coming to inspect the unit. New uniforms are issued, and everything is cleaned and polished. "Everyone is peevish and touchy, we do not take kindly to all this polishing, much less to parades. Such things exasperate a soldier more than the frontline." When the kaiser arrives, Bäumer is disappointed to see that he is a short man with a thin voice. The kaiser's departure precipitates a bitter discussion among Bäumer and his friends in which they speculate on whether the kaiser is responsible for the war. Bäumer thinks that war is wrong, stating that while both sides would make their case, neither side has a legitimate cause. Tjaden is persistent in his questioning of what constitutes a country or a state and succeeds in making some important observations. "'Gendarmes, police, taxes, that's your State.'" Tjaden further responds that the "state" is not made up of the ordinary citizen, who would never elect to go to war, but, rather, the rulers. "I had never seen a Frenchman before I came here, and it will be just the same with the majority of Frenchmen as regards us. They weren't asked about it any more than we were.'" The soldier concludes that the kaiser's motivation for wanting war is purely self-serving, fueled by his desire to make himself historically important. "And every full-grown emperor requires at least one war, otherwise he wouldn't become famous."

Bäumer's company is sent to the front once again. While they are traveling, the narrator offers additional graphic descriptions of the ravages of war. "Here hang bits of uniform, and somewhere else is plastered a bloody mess that was once a human limb." During the fighting, Bäumer is pinned in a shell hole and separated from his friends, causing him to panic. Despite his efforts to the contrary, imagining a threatening scenario, he cannot console himself. "Here I am alone and almost helpless in the dark—perhaps two other eyes have been watching me for a long while from another shell-hole in front of me, and a bomb lies ready to blow me to pieces." As enemy troops pass by, he lies face down, pretending to be dead, all the while reproaching himself. Bäumer eventually recognizes the voices of his comrades and is immediately relieved of his feeling of isolation. "I am no longer a shuddering speck of existence, alone in the darkness;—I belong to them and they to me, we all share the same fear and the same life, we are nearer than lovers, in a simpler, harder way...." Once again, Remarque underscores the only positive theme in *All Quiet*— the camaraderie of war that compensates for the loss of home and family. After recognizing the voices, Bäumer attempts to crawl out of the hole but is gripped with fear when he discovers he has lost his sense of direction in the apocalyptic landscape. "The confusion of shell-holes now seems so bewildering that I can no longer tell in my agitation which way I should go." He retreats to a large trench where he slips down into the water, hiding in the mud, and where another body jumps into the hole with him, producing a wave of abject fear. Without thinking,

Bäumer stabs him. "I strike madly home, and feel only how the body suddenly convulses, then becomes limp, and collapses." Because of the impending dawn and the encroaching daylight, Bäumer is forced to stay in the trench to protect himself, all the while afraid to look at the dark figure that lies there beside him. With the onset of morning, the gurgling sounds from the dark figure stops and, to Bäumer's horror, the man begins to move. "He is dead, I say to myself, he must be dead. . . . Then the head tries to raise itself, for a moment the groaning becomes louder, his forehead sinks back upon his arm." The body in the trench, it turns out, is a French soldier. Immediately filled with remorse for his actions, Bäumer attempts to comfort the soldier while bandaging him and giving him water. "'I want to help you, Comrade, camerade, camerade, camerade,' eagerly repeating the word, to make him understand." But despite Bäumer's best efforts, the soldier dies, slowly, for the stab wounds he has sustained are beyond repair. The soldier's death he has caused will continue to weigh heavily on Bäumer. His remorse is so pronounced that the dying man unknowingly retaliates psychologically, exacting a heavy price from his murderer. "This dying man has time with him, he has an invisible dagger with which he stabs me; Time and my thoughts." Once the French soldier expires, Bäumer's inner torment only increases as he imagines the soldier's wife. "My state is getting worse, I can no longer control my thoughts." Bäumer speaks to the dead man, explaining that he did not want to kill him. "But you were only an idea to me before, an abstraction that lived in my mind. . . . It was that abstraction I stabbed. But now, for the first time, I see you are a man like me." As Bäumer searches through the soldier's wallet, he finds out that his name is Gérard Duval, that he earned his living as a printer and leaves behind him a wife and child. Bäumer is deeply aggrieved that he has been reduced to murdering a fellow human being. He also realizes that he will never be able to write to the man's family, though he had promised himself he would.

By afternoon, Bäumer has regained his composure so that his thoughts recur to his own perilous predicament. "I think no more of the dead man, he is of no consequence to me now. With one bound the lust to live flares up again and everything that has filled my thoughts goes down before it." As Bäumer attempts to crawl along as noiselessly as possible, he reaches Kat and Albert, who have been looking for him and have a stretcher waiting for him. The three, however, are forced to jump into a trench to avoid getting hit. Thoughts of the dead soldier return to haunt Bäumer, but his friends quickly calm him, explaining that such barbarous actions are the essence of war. **Chapter 9** concludes with Sergeant Oellrich's rifle ringing out "sharp and dry."

Chapter 10 begins with Bäumer's unit arriving in an abandoned village in order to guard a supply depot. It is an easy assignment that affords comfortable accommodations and abundant food and supplies, as they take up residence in a dugout reinforced with concrete. "So we zealously set to work to create an idyll—an idyll of eating and sleeping, of course. Indeed, the description of their temporary living situation sounds almost ideal. "There is plenty to be found in the town. Albert and I find a mahogany bed which can be taken to pieces, with a sky of blue silk and a lace coverlet." Bäumer and his friends relax and eat well for three weeks. After discovering two young pigs, they prepare a feast, complete with fresh vegetables and potato cakes. Their hospitality even extends to visitors when a couple of wireless operators arrive, whom they feed and entertain by singing and playing the piano. All is not ideal, however, as the reality of war inexorably reaches them. "The observation balloons have spotted the smoke from the chimney, and shells start to drop on us." Once this happens, the singing comes to a halt when the piano is hit, and Bäumer must keep ducking while he attempts to flip the potato pancakes. Nonetheless, the soldiers are not deterred and continue their feast with coffee, cognac, rum, and fine cigars. Even a small gray cat is admitted to their small company while outside the signs of war abound. "Burning houses stand out like torches against the night. Shells lumber across and crash down."

The soldiers receive orders to return to the front, though Bäumer and Albert are determined not to relinquish all the luxuries to which they have grown accustomed. "Two big motor lorries take us away. . . . Nevertheless, Albert and I erect on top our four-poster bed complete with blue canopy, mattress, and two lace coverlets. And behind it at the head is stowed a bag full of choice edibles." They even take the cat with them, stowed in a parrot cage with her saucer.

A few days later, they are sent to evacuate a village and are given a grim account of a pathetic community, ripped from their homes and left destitute. We are given a glimpse of the far-reaching tentacles of war that eventually wreak havoc on everyone. "On the way we meet the fleeing inhabitants trundling their goods and chattels along with them in wheel-barrows, perambulators, and on their backs. Their figures are bent, their faces full of grief, despair, haste and resignation." Once the town is evacuated, the French begin their bombardment, while Kropp and Bäumer are wounded and at least get to lie next to each other on their way to the hospital. They arrive to a hospital where the most grim of conditions prevail. Bäumer gives a vivid account of the callous treatment imparted by compassionless doctors followed by a detailed discussion of the amputation industry. "I am frightened and think quickly what I ought to do; for everyone knows that the surgeons in the dressing-stations amputate on the slightest provocation. Under the great pressure of business that is much simpler than complicated patching." Fortunately for Bäumer, his wounds are deemed minor, and after a piece of shell is removed from his leg, he receives a plaster cast. Kropp is more seriously hurt and vows to end his life if he loses his leg. Both men, however, want to escape and find their friends. The next morning, they are placed side by side on stretchers and wait in the rain on a train platform. Through Bäumer's maneuvering, they bribe the sergeant major with cigars so that they can ride together. Once inside the train, Bäumer is afraid to lie down with his dirty clothes on the crisp white linen bedsheets, but the Red Cross nurse tells him not to worry about it.

During the journey, Kropp suffers a high fever. Fearful that they will be separated because of Kropp's condition, Bäumer devises a way of altering the reading on his thermometer so that it too registers a fever. "I stick the thermometer under my arm at a slant, and flip it steadily with my forefinger. . . . I send it up to 100.2°. But that is not enough. A match held cautiously near to it brings it up to 101.6 °." This simple deception reveals the strong bonds of friendship that develop in wartime. When the train stops, both men are sent to the same hospital. Luckily, Josef Hammacher is in their ward. He is proud to have a "shooting license." Hammacher's certificate states that he cannot be held responsible for his actions, for he is a deranged man, a fact that comes in handy when Bäumer flings a bottle in the hallway in order to get the nuns to close the door and shut out the sound of their prayers. When the hospital inspector comes by to investigate a few hours later, Hammacher takes responsibility for throwing the bottle, and the affair is immediately dropped.

Most of the soldiers in the hospital are close to death. Bäumer watches as Franz Wächter dies of an agonizing septic wound. Though Bäumer rings for a nurse to help Franz, whose bandage is leaking, no one responds. The nun serving as night nurse is tired of their constant demands to be made more comfortable and so ignores Bäumer's repeated pleas for attention. Though she finally arrives and bandages Franz, the dying man now looks deathly sick, his face "sharp and yellow." One nun, Sister Libertine, is able to summon some sympathy for the men, and Bäumer singles her out for praise, "this marvellous sister, who spreads good cheer through the whole wing even when she can only be seen in the distance." Quickly returning to the subject of Franz, Bäumer reveals that one day the wounded man is taken away to the Dead Room and never seen again. Another severely wounded patient, a curly-haired soldier named Peter, is able to return from this lamentable location, the first to have accomplished such an amazing feat. "And even Josef has to admit that it is the first time he has ever known of such a thing."

Bäumer is operated on during this time, and the surgeon's secretary makes a dismal prophecy that his broken bones will not properly heal. According to Josef, surgeons are fond of this diagnosis, as it gives them an opportunity to operate and create a crippling condition, leaving the patient with club feet. As for Albert Kropp, his leg has been amputated, with devastating effects on the man. "Now he hardly speaks anymore. Once he says he will shoot himself the first time he can get hold of his revolver again." Bäumer then discusses two blind men who are admitted to their room. In desperation, one of them attempts suicide by driving a fork into his heart. By the next morning, this same man suffers from lockjaw.

As Bäumer hobbles around on crutches, he comments on what he witnesses on the other floors. Just below him are the abdominal and spine cases as well as the head wounds and double amputations. Expounding on the vulnerability of these wounded soldiers, Bäumer's commentary turns to the humanity that is eclipsed by the terrors of war, even in a hospital environment where the purported occupation is to heal the sick and wounded. "A man cannot realize that above such shattered bodies there are still human faces in which life goes its daily round. And this is only one hospital, one single station. . . . It must all be lies and of no account when the culture of a thousand years could not prevent this stream of blood being poured out. . . ."

Chapter 10 concludes with Bäumer going to get a therapeutic massage, as he has done for several weeks. Albert Kropp is to be sent to an institute specializing in artificial limbs. Though Bäumer is still depressed, he believes that he and his friends have at least succeeded in preventing Albert's suicide and have returned the amputee to a state where he is once again alive to his surroundings. "But now he is over the worst of it, and he often looks on while we play skat." Bäumer, too, has received convalescent leave and, as he tells us, the return home is again painful. His mother has grown increasingly more feeble and does not want to let go of her son when it is time for him to return to the front lines once again.

Chapter 11 begins with a dismal awareness of the passage of time, for though it was winter when Bäumer first arrived, it is now spring, and unlike the natural world which renews itself in cycles, the conditions of war are as obtrusive and overwhelming as ever. War has had a leveling effect that produces a new set of injustices. "Distinctions, breeding, education are changed, are almost blotted out and hardly recognizable any longer. Sometimes they give an advantage for profiting by a situation; but they also bring consequences along with them, in that they arouse prejudices which have to be overcome." This equalizing effect is a condition of war in which all energies are narrowly focused on the necessity of sheer survival. Though Bäumer reflects on the superficiality of their existence, it is the sense of camaraderie that has given solace and helped his fellow soldiers "escape the abyss of solitude." Bäumer is quick to remind us of an inescapable irony, namely that there are "aberrational" moments when human emotions erupt and threaten to destroy their fight for survival. "Those are the dangerous moments. They show us that the adjustment is only artificial, that it is not simple rest, but sharpest struggle for rest." As Bäumer points out, their fellowship of survival is actually quite primitive and, on the surface, their lives resemble that of an aboriginal community on which civilization has not encroached, despite the fact they lack the essential spiritual component found in such native groups. "In the outward form of life we are hardly distinguishable from Bushmen; but whereas the latter can be so always, because they are so truly, and at best may develop further by exertion of their spiritual forces, with us it is the reverse;—our inner forces are not exerted towards regeneration, but toward degeneration."

As time passes, Bäumer is reminded of how life continues to be wasted and how emotional well-being breaks down while serving on the front lines. To illustrate his point, he relates the story of Detering's madness. A farmer who consistently longs to return home, Detering has apparently seen a lone cherry tree that reminds him of his own orchard. One evening he breaks off a few branches for himself and when he returns he begins packing his personal items with the excuse that he cannot sleep. In an effort to distract him from his ostensible plan to desert, Bäumer asks him for a piece of bread which, under ordinary circumstances, Detering would be reluctant to part with. When he hands it over without any protest, Bäumer's suspicions are aroused, for he recognizes the signs of determination Detering unknowingly displays. "When these peasants are excited they have a curious expression, a mixture of cow and yearning god, half stupid and haft rapt." When Detering manages to escape the next evening, his absence is noted at roll call and, a week later, there is news that he has been caught by the "despicable military police." Nothing further is heard of the deserter. Nevertheless, as Bäumer comments, these inexplicable turn of events happen, borne of seething emotions, "as from an overheated boiler."

Returning to life in the trenches, Bäumer notes that the network of tunnels has been so extensively compromised from being continually bombarded with artillery that they can no longer sustain a semblance of proper trench warfare. The German army has begun to collapse, as it cannot successfully confront the Allied troops that are well supplied and provided with reinforcements. "There's too much corned beef and white wheaten bread. Too many new guns. Too many aeroplanes." Muller has been shot, but before dying he bequeaths his yellow leather boots to Bäumer, the same boots that originally belonged to their long-deceased friend, Kemmerich. Bäumer recounts how the remaining German soldiers are weak, starving, and overcome with dysentery. He grimly notes that the new recruits are automatically marked for sacrifice. "They understand nothing about warfare, they simply go on and let themselves be shot down." The soldiers are without hope, and Kat's story of his travels from Vosges to Flanders only reinforces the feelings of despair. Many disreputable military doctors, all too willing to declare wounded men fit for service and ready to be returned to active duty, are in attendance. "[E]very soldier some time during his hundreds of inspections falls into the clutches of these countless hero-grabbers who pride themselves on changing as many C3's and B3's as possible into A1's." The soldiers are so weary of the war that they function without thought or feeling, like robots; they feel the only way they will leave the fighting is to be dead or hospitalized. "Trenches, hospitals, the common grave—there are no other possibilities."

During one attack, Bertinck, an officer the young soldiers admire, is cut down. Bertinck is portrayed as heroic for when the soldiers open fire from their trench and when it appears they are outmanned and outgunned, Bertinck crawls out of the hole to fire on the flame throwers, sustaining a bullet wound to the chest. Though injured, he continues undeterred and successfully fires on the enemy. At the same time, Leer is also hit and quickly bleeds to death in the trenches. It is a senseless waste, as Bäumer comments: "What use is it to him now that he was such a good mathematician at school?"

The months drag on until it is the summer of 1918, one of the few specific historical details offered by the narrative. Though the end of the war is by all accounts near at hand, these last days are horrific. Still, the soldiers yearn for life, as their intense suffering is contrasted with signs of nature's regeneration. "Never has life in its niggardliness seemed to us so desirable as now;—the red poppies in the meadows round our billets, the smooth beetles on the blades of grass, the warm evenings in the cool, dim rooms. . . ." During one of the war's final skirmishes, Kat is hit in the leg by a bullet and is seriously injured. Facing dangerous obstacles, Bäumer puts his injured friend on his back to carry him to the nearest medical station, miserable at the thought that he may never see Kat again. When Bäumer arrives at the station, Kat is already dead, having sustained another bullet wound to the head. The loss of his best friend is painful. **Chapter 11** concludes with one numbing thought alone: "Only the Militiaman Stanislaus Katczinsky has died. Then I know nothing more."

By autumn 1918 Bäumer is the only one of the classmates still alive, amazed that he has survived this long, when all of his comrades have perished. He also believes that if a peace agreement is not reached soon, a violent revolt will take place. "If it again proves an illusion, then they will break up; hope is high, it cannot be taken away again without an upheaval." As **Chapter 12** opens, Bäumer has been given a two-week period of rest, because he has succumbed to gas poisoning. He uses the time to reflect on his wartime losses and lament the pitiful condition of a young generation that has lost all hope and spirit. At the same time, Bäumer is worried about his own future, for he does not have the advantages of the older generation that sent him to war, the same authority figures that were already established in their homes and occupations before the war. "We will be superfluous even to ourselves, we will grow older, a few will adapt themselves, some others will merely submit, and most will be bewildered;—the years will pass by and in the end we shall fall into ruin."

In the last two paragraphs of *All Quiet on the Western Front*, an unidentified narrator reports that Bäumer is dead, but from the peaceful look on his face, has clearly not suffered. An epitaph has been written for Bäumer, killed only one month before the Armistice. Ironically, on this particular day, "all was quiet on the Western Front" and Bäumer appeared almost relieved that the end had finally come.

Critical Views

BRIAN MURDOCH ON *ALL QUIET ON THE WESTERN FRONT* AS A WEIMAR ANTIWAR NOVEL

That a historical event of the magnitude of the First World War, which cost around ten million lives from most nations of the world, could be encapsulated to any extent in a novel the paperback edition of which has little more than two hundred pages is an achievement in itself.[12] The fact that the body of the novel is a convincingly presented first-person narrative means that it *does* still need to be spelled out that Bäumer is not Remarque, who drew without doubt upon his own experiences in the war and at home in Osnabrück. But *Im Westen nichts Neues* is a work of fiction, and most importantly it has only one character. With two small but significant exceptions, the young soldier Paul Bäumer delivers the work directly to the reader, and therefore everything we see or hear is through him. It testifies to Remarque's skill that Bäumer remains consistent throughout the work, and it is Bäumer's character and background that dictates the style.[13] The choice of a narrator is significant; because Bäumer, drafted in 1916, was still a schoolboy in 1914, he bears no personal responsibility for the war itself, nor indeed does he understand much about it. Equally, Remarque does not permit him any prescience (although of course he speculates) about what happens *after* the war. This has an effect on the way in which other figures are presented to us, and criticism has been leveled at the book for the apparent one-sidedness of some of the characters encountered, or for the limited view of the fighting troops. But since they are all presented through Bäumer, his close friends would clearly be in far sharper focus than an anonymous and unpleasant major, or even an attractive French girl met on one occasion only. Bäumer would in reality have been unlikely to know the names of either of them. Nor would he have had much of a view of the war beyond company level, and his immediate experience with senior or even junior officers would be limited. The most senior officer glimpsed in the work is in fact Kaiser Wilhelm, when he comes to review the troops, but apart from one major and his own second lieutenant, Bäumer mentions no one else above the noncommissioned ranks. *Im Westen nichts Neues*, and to an extent the sequel, seem by this approach to claim the advantages of a diary—that is, its immediacy—with none of the drawbacks of a precise chronology, and Bäumer (and Birkholz in *Der Wig zurück*) present their thoughts, experiences, and reflections directly to the reader.[14]

The individual private soldier Paul Bäumer nevertheless sees himself for most of the novel as part of a group, so that it is the first person plural that predominates much of the work, and the move away from it at the end to Bäumer as an individual gains in significance thereby. Nor, of course, must we forget Remarque as the (concealed) structuring author behind the character, controlling the work as a whole in the variation in chapter lengths, or in the balance of action and periods of inaction, of reported discussion and private reflection. Remarque allows Bäumer to send signals to the reader to consider how single events need to be multiplied by thousands, for example, or indications that a particular train of thought will be able to be taken to a logical conclusion only after the war.

It is also sometimes overlooked that *Im Westen nichts Neues* is not a contemporary account of the First World War. Although both novels contain episodes based upon historical reality,[15] *Im Westen nichts Neues* was not written in 1918, but in 1928, recreating within the Weimar Republic events that had happened ten or more years before, even if those events were part of the experience of many of those living in the new postwar German state. *Im Westen niche Neues* is historical fiction, and so is *Das Weg zurück*, although by the time of the latter, the sense that history was moving on was more apparent.[16] That Remarque chose to set the two novels during and just after the war itself means that they cannot be historically reflective in themselves, but both raise questions to which the narrator was never in a position to give answers.

The burden of finding answers is thus placed upon the reader, whether in 1930 or in the present, and wherever he or she may be responding to the work.[17] In the first instance the target audience was the Weimar Republic itself, because both novels reflect the shared history of those reaching maturity in a postwar Germany that was already beginning to look insecure. But they were addressed, also, to the contemporary world, sending out a specifically pacifist message to Germany's former enemies. Beside these two time levels—that of the action and that of the contemporary reception—stands a third, the time of the present reader. They are addressed also to an international posterity and remain important in their general implications.

There are two places in *Im Westen nichts Neues* in which Bäumer is not in control of the narrative: There is a prefatory statement by the author that was omitted in some translations and appears in others with a significant variation from the text of the first German edition. It may be cited . . . [in] the translation by A. W. Wheen, who included it in full in his 1929 translation:

[This book is to be neither an accusation nor a confession, and least of all an adventure, for death is not an adventure to those who stand face to face with it. It will try simply to tell of a generation of men who, even though they may have escaped its shells, were destroyed by the war.]

The statement in its original form was necessary because there were many examples of literature that did present the war in that light. More importantly though, it categorizes the work as a *Bericht*, a report, reminding us that although the fictive narrator would have been dead for ten years when the book appeared, other soldiers had survived. As a parallel with this opening statement, the final half-dozen lines of the novel are spoken by a new third-person narrator within the historical fictionality of the book, commenting on the death of Bäumer.

It was argued early in the criticism of the novel that the presentation of the war by a single individual could not portray a valid picture of the war. There are various responses to this: one is that the first person in the novel is, as indicated, frequently the plural *wir*, so that Bäumer speaks for other soldiers and their experiences. Furthermore, even the notion of "other soldiers" can mean a variety of things, ranging from just Bäumer and Katczinsky (Kat), his mentor, to his immediate groups of school or platoon comrades, to his company, to the German army, or even the Germans as a whole. Refining it again, it might refer to the ordinary German soldier, or indeed to the ordinary soldier as such. Remarque permits Bäumer and his comrades to stress their representative status by pointing out that most of the soldiers of all countries are also ordinary people, and also by introducing overtly what might be seen as a multiplication factor at key points. Thus Bäumer says of the teacher, Kantorek, who had bullied them into signing up: "Es gab ja Tausende von Kantoreks" (18, there were thousands of Kantoreks), and more significantly towards the end of the novel, of the military hospital, which shows the true measure of war: "es gibt Hunderttausende in Deutschland, Hunderttausende in Frankreich, Hunderttausende in Russland . . ." (177, there are hundreds of thousands of them in Germany, hundreds of thousands of them in France, hundreds of thousands of them in Russia).

The *Froschperspektive* need not, then, be as restricted as it might appear. But the narrator is also an individual; wars may be expressed in terms of the often unimaginably large numbers of those who fought or were killed, but such statistics are always made up of individuals. Remarque reduces the *wir* element gradually throughout the work in parallel to what was a war of attrition that ultimately reached the single individual, when at the end Paul Bäumer is not just left alone, but is thrown onto his own inner resources without support from any side. The ultimate expression of Bäumer's existentialist realization of the nature of life in the face of the extreme situation of war links this work with Remarque's oeuvre as a whole.

The fictional time of the novel begins in 1917, well after the outbreak of the war, and the reader is aware of time— more specifically of the seasons—passing until October 1918.

Bäumer's own thoughts and conversations with others take the reader back to earlier periods, but in the fictional present the deadly monotony and constant attrition is completely established. The first chapter begins with *wir*, which refers on this occasion to a company of 150 men, just back from what was supposed to be a quiet sector after heavy losses, and with only eighty survivors. The battle has not been an important one, and the reason for the losses is casually put: . . .

[But then, on the very last day we were taken by surprise by long-range shelling from the heavy artillery. The English guns kept on pounding our position, so we lost a lot of men, and only eighty of us came back.]

Notes

12. There is a large body of secondary literature on the novel (some cited elsewhere in this chapter), and it is usually discussed in studies of war novels as such: George Parfitt's *Fiction of the First World War* (London: Faber, 1988) is a study of English-language novels with reference otherwise only to Remarque, Ernst Jünger, Jules Romains, and Henri Barbusse, and this is true too (minus Romains) of Bernard Bergonzi, *Heroes' Twilight: A Study of the Literature of the Great War* 2d ed. (London: Macmillan, 1980). There are monograph-length studies of *Im Westen nichts Neues* by the present writer, *Remarque: Im Westen nichts Neues*, as well as by Firda, *All Quiet*, and Rüter, *Bestseller*. There are various papers in the *Jahrbuch* 10 (2000), and many studies compare the work with other novels of the war: Helmut Liedloff, "Two War Novels," *Revue de Littérature Comparée* 42 (1968): 390–406 (with Hemingway); Holger M. Klein, "Dazwischen Niemandsland: *Im Westen nichts Neues* and *Her Privata We*, in *Grossbritannien und Deutschland: Festschrift für John W. P. Bourke*, ed. Ortwin Kuhn (Munich: Goldmann, 1974), 488–512 (with Manning); Holger M. Klein, "Grundhaltung und Feindbilder bei Remarque, Céline und Hemingway," *Krieg und Literatur/War and Literature* 1 (1989): 7–22. Some studies are less useful than others: David J. Ulbrich, "A Male-Conscious Critique of Erich Maria Remarque's *All Quiet on the Western Front*," *Journal of Men's Studies* 3 (1995): 229–40 is not enlightening. Given the clarity of the novel it is intriguing to note the continued production of "study guides" in English, which do little more than provide a detailed plot summary (*Cliffs Notes*, 1965;. Monarch Notes, 1966; Coles Notes, 1984; Sparknotes, 2002). See in German however the rather different introductions by Peter Bekes,

Erich Maria Remarque: Im Westen nichts Neues (Munich: Oldenbourg, 1998), and Reiner Poppe, *Erich Maria Remarque: Im Westen nichts Neues* (Hollfeld: Beyer, 1998). An adapted and abridged version of the English text was published for foreign students of the English language (such has it become part of the English canon): *Remarque: All Quiet on the Western Front,* adapted by Colin Swatridge (London: Macmillan, 1987).

13. As noted by Rowley, "Journalism into Fiction," 108. Rowley also indicates the importance of the chapter division and their varying lengths on 109. Rowley's reference, however, to a "curiously unrealistic cross-section of the fighting-troops" (109) is surely explained by the fact that this, too, is dictated, by Bäumer's "frog's eye view," a term Rowley cites, 108.

14. An early subtitle was "Aus den Tagebüchern des Freiwilligen Georg Bäumers" (From the Diaries of the Volunteer Soldier Georg Bäumer—the name was changed later, too). See Schneider, *Text, Edition, Entsuhung,* 463. See my paper "Paul Bäumer's Diary" in Murdoch, Ward, and Sergeant, *Remarque Against War,* 1–23.

15. The debate about the actual reality of the presentation of the war in the novel has continued in various forms since the first objections by those critics who wanted it to be autobiographical. See Günter Hartung, "Zum Wahrheitsgehalt des Romans *Im Westen nichts Neues,*" *Jahrbuch* 1 (1991): 5–17. See also my "Paul Bäumer's Diary." Paul Fussell, *The Great War and Modern Memory* (London: Oxford UP, 1977), 183, counters the notion that the work is as "real and intimate" as letters from the front.

16. Hans-Harald Müller makes the point clearly in "Politics and the War Novel," in *German Writers and Politics 1918–39,* ed. Richard Dove and Stephen Lamb (London: Macmillan, 1992), 103–20, esp. 112.

17. On Remarque's discourse technique, already apparent in these early novels, see Heinrich Placke on the works of the 1950s: *Die Chiffren des Utopischen: Zum literarischen Gehalt der politischen 50er-Jahre-Romane Remarques* (Göttingen: Vandenhoek and Ruprecht, 2004).

BRIAN MURDOCH ON REMARQUE AND HOMER

One response to Remarque which deserves more attention, however, falls into a quite distinct literary mode, that of parody. *Vor Troja nichts Neues* was published by the Brunnen-Verlag in Berlin in 1930 under the pseudonym 'Emil Marius Requark' and it sold relatively well. As with the other works mentioned, it depended for its sales upon knowledge of the original, and imitated the Ullstein dust jacket for Remarque's book in detail, adding a parody version of Walther von Molo's much-quoted endorsement of Remarque's book as a monument to the unknown warrior, a comment used to the full by Ullstein in their extensive publicity for *Im Westen nichts Neues*. Rüter has commented that commercial considerations played a particularly strong part in this case, but although this may well be true, parody is the literary form in which one work necessarily rides upon another.[7] That this may have commercial implications in any case is even from time to time made explicit as part of the humour of the parody. H. N. Beard and D. C. Kenney's parody of Tolkien's *Lord of the Rings* begins 'This book is predominantly concerned with making money, and from its pages a reader may learn much about the character and the literary integrity of the authors.'[8] It might also be recalled that Remarque's book was itself at the centre of an extremely high-powered advertising campaign.

Parody is a complex form. A parody may constitute a sharp form of criticism, drawing attention usually by comic exaggeration to flaws in the original, but it may at the same time continue to show a regard for that original. Indeed, the creation of a parody acknowledges that the original is sufficiently well-known for the imitation to be worthwhile. Its dependence upon a known original may mean that when the original is obscured, parody itself weakens, although this need not mean that it, too, will be consigned to a similar obscurity. *Joseph Andrews* survives, as does *Northanger Abbey*, but not all of Pope. *Vor Troja nichts Neues* does indeed raise questions about Remarque and his work, and indeed about the marketing of that work. At the same time, though, it raises questions supplementary to those put by *Im Westen nichts Neues*. It is not, in Rüter's terms, only or even primarily a 'Gegenschrift', and it is not only a parody of Remarque. In some respects it is a parody of Homer through the medium of Remarque, and Homer and the heroic ideal has served as a target in both wars. The connexion with Homer, giving us a work that depends upon two literary models for the appreciation of its humour that have remained extremely well known, may well serve to save this work. The critical 'Gegenschriften' by Kropp and others are long forgotten, and have little to say beyond the documentation of a one-time literary furore. This is true particularly of those works endorsing the 'Stahlhelm' philosophy, though Friedlaender's attack, too, soon sank beneath the weight of its own cleverness. Remarque became part of world literature very quickly, and the evidence of Evadne Price's title is not insignificant. The parody is still worthy of consideration, for all that the reception of *Vor Troja nichts Neues* is not necessarily the same now as when it was written. It may be, as some critics have considered, that the work was intended as an attack on Remarque's pacificism, and it certainly accuses him of commercialism. But, there is sufficient ambiguity in the work—something not infrequent in parody—for the work to be taken by the modern reader as an attack no less on Homer or, indeed, on war, than on Remarque. The last line of the work, the conclusion of a spoof 'Nachwort' on the authorship of this supposedly ancient text, comments that the whole thing is 'die Ehrenrettung des Thersites'. The line may have some truth in it.

It is presumed that Max Joseph Wolff is the man behind the pseudonym, although few bibliographies attribute the work, and there is a double distancing in a work published under a quite well concealed pseudonym which is then narrated by a different persona. Wolff was a literary historian and author of works on Shakespeare and Molière, who published other parodies for the same publishing house, either as 'A. Perspicax' or as 'Allemand Daudet'. His parodies include a work on the French in the Rhineland in the style of Daudet which was translated into English in 1922.[9]

Those critics who have discussed the work at all tend to be dismissive of *Vor Troja nichts Neues*. For Rüter it is simply a 'Travestie', for Alan Bance a 'reputedly feeble skit', for C. R. Owen (who seems not to like parodies anyway) merely 'not very good'. Christine Barker and Rex Last give a brief summary of what the latter elsewhere calls a 'wicked parody', but conclude that it is directed against Remarque's pacifist tendencies and the personal vanity of his implicit claim to be the 'sole repository of the whole truth about the armed conflict on the Western front'.[10] Whether this is a sufficient judgement of the work is open to question. It depends in part at least on the complete identification of the narrator of the parody—the Greek Thersites—with Remarque, and the acceptance of Homer's, or more accurately Agamemnon's, view of the Thersites of the *Iliad*.

Thersites himself provides an interesting touchstone. In the second book of the *Iliad* he is the common soldier, described by Homer as an ugly, balding and bow-legged trouble-maker, who makes a speech against Agamemnon, accusing him of prolonging the war for profit and of insulting Achilles, who is also not regarded favourably. For this speech he is beaten by Odysseus and becomes a laughing-stock. Clearly he is intended to be a foil for the heroic central figures and this is the way most critics have tended to regard him, treating his role, too, as a comic one. Other critics, however, have pointed out that Thersites's case is not so simple. He may be a figure of disorder, but he is speaking the truth. He recognises—thus K. J. Atchity—'as others apparently do not, the full implications and dangers of the quarrel' between Achilles and Agamemnon. He is punished, broadly speaking, because 'Iliadic society is not democratic'.[11]

The question of shifting reception is an important one. Homer presumably intended no sympathy for Thersites, any more than the anonymous writer of the *Chanson de Roland* intended sympathy for Ganelon, at least on the superficial level. Ganelon, we are told, is a villain, and he is tagged throughout as 'Ganelon, who did the treachery'. A modern audience might, while not approving of Ganelon's methods, at least understand his dissatisfaction both with a war that has been going on for far too long and with the insufferably arrogant Roland. Ganelon the traitor and Thersites the boor, both tired of an over-long war, must surely now be viewed in the light of more recent events.

It is hardly surprising that Thersites, the representative of the 'Fußvolk', the poor bloody infantry, should take the centre of the stage in more recent times. If *Im Westen nichts Neues* has the common soldier as the primary figure in a drama of the Western front, it is logical that Thersites, too, should be used to reverse the heroic ideal extracted for so long from Greek writing and from Homer in particular. The point is made seriously in other works. Ernst Glaeser's *Jahrgang 1902* shows, for example, a boy growing up during the First World War, and the final chapter shows him learning Homer in terms of a concept of heroism that he knows is no longer valid, and reading about heroic feasts in the hungry final stages of the blockade: . . .

The attack on pre-1914 pedagogics, especially in their preoccupation with the classical heroic ideal, is not unfamiliar elsewhere in Weimar literature, and a more democratic view than that of the *Iliad* is beginning to make itself felt. . . .

. . . *Vor Troja nichts Neues* is able as a parody of *Im Westen nichts Neues* to raise questions about that novel. Wolff's book, though, also uses the externals and the context of Remarque's work to provide a basis for a reversal of the heroic ideals in Homer. Anachronism is a useful comic device, and the receptive overlap for the reader of a structure belonging to a novel about the Western Front and the characters and places of Homeric Greece and Troy makes for a double comedy, and the work is genuinely funny, one of the hallmarks of parody; the national anthem of the Greeks is "Hellas, Hellas über alles", for example. *Vor Troja nichts Neues* attacks Ullstein's marketing strategy, mocks specific and easily identified elements of Remarque's narrative, and may also have been aimed at his pacifism. But whatever the reception may have been in 1930, the central figure and narrator is now able to engage the reader's sympathy, at least in a picaresque sense. The reception of the work may be affected by a lesser familiarity with Homer than was normal in the 1930s, but at the same time the reception now cannot but reflect the changed attitude to war expressed in novels like *Catch 22*, an attitude which began, in fact, with the appearance of novels like that of Remarque. Thersites's points in the parody tend to be as valid as those made by Remarque through Bäumer, even if the motivation is a little different. The complete and unconcealed cynicism of Thersites is often perfectly acceptable to a modern audience and the effect is undeniably entertaining.

Notes

7. Emil Marius Requark, *Vor Troja nichts Neues*, Berlin 1930. At least 30,000 copies were printed. The text is cited in the present paper with page numbers in parentheses following. It has to be remembered that Remarque's war book was not the only best-seller of the period, even for Ullstein, who also produced Gunther Plüschow's *Die Abenteuer des Fliegers von Tsingtau*, Berlin 1927, a new edition with an added conclusion of a text from 1916, which sold well over half a million copies. See D. R. Richards, *The German Bestseller in the 20th Century*, Berne 1968, p. 55.

8. Henry N. Beard and Douglas C. Kenney, *Bored of the Rings*, New York, 1969. It has even been translated, as *Der Herr de Augenringe*, Munich 1983.

9. See Owen, *Remarque*, pp. 137f. Wolff published, as A. Perspicax, *Des Rattenfänger von Europa, Aristide Briand*, Berlin 1931, and earlier, as Allemand Daudet, *Der Meisterboxer*, Berlin 1923. Geoffrey E. Hare's *Alphonse Daudet: A Critical Bibliography*, London 1979, II, p. 130 refers to a work under the same name published as *Tartarin am Rhein* and then translated in 1922. The spelling of the writer's middle name varies.

10. Rüter, *Remarque*, p. 162; Owen, *Remarque*, p. 138; A. F. C. Bance, '*Im Westen nichts Neues*: A Bestseller in Context', *MLR*, 72 (1977), 360; Christine Barker and Rex Last, *Erich Maria Remarque*, London 1979, p. 41 (for whom the work is a 'slight but acid parody'). In his 'The "Castration" of Erich Maria Remarque', *Quinquereme*, 2 (1979), 11, Rex Last refers to the 'wicked parody' as possibly from the hand of Friedlaender, though he is aware that there is no proof. The styles are very different indeed, though there are possible points in common.

11. Thersites appears in the *Iliad*, II, 212–46. For a traditional view of him, see C. M. Bowra, *Homer*, London 1972, and for the view that the incident is comic, C. A. Trypanis, *The Homeric Epics*, Warminster 1977, p. 23 and Cedric H. Whitman, *Homer and the Heroic Tradition*, Cambridge, Mass. 1967, p. 261. Kenneth Jon Atchity discusses him in *Homer's Iliad: The Shield of Memory*, Carbondale/Edwardsville 1978, pp. 126f., and see also the introduction to Martin Hammond's new translation of the *Iliad*, Harmondsworth 1967, p. 20.

A.F. Bance on the Novel's Best-seller Status

Remarque capitalizes on the bare *Fronterlebnis*; for the authenticity which the experience lends his novel needs no further embellishment. There is an interesting parallel with the way that Hitler's speeches and career capitalized on his front-line experience as the ultimate legitimation of his message, superseding politics, for 'are not feelings, unlike the complexities of economics or politics, something Everyman can understand and judge and share?'[1] In these terms, lack of documentation means a *greater* authenticity in the novel, not less, and paradoxically the documentary obsession of other war-writers can be seen simply as obscuring this authenticity of their personal statements. There is very little in *Im Westen* to inhibit the reader's response; the lowest common denominator is invariably found. Paul Bäumer, the hero, though not lacking in educational background (and the conventional artistic aspirations of the *Abiturient*) deliberately assumes and even exaggerates the ignorance of the humblest ranker. Remarque reduces him totally to the passive object of official decisions. There is a great deal of popular attraction as well as some truth, in the view of the war as a social leveller.[2] In the front line education and class confer few advantages. There are not many other successful works which exploit this aspect of the war so thoroughly. . . .

It may well be that the undocumentary vagueness that characterizes *Im Westen*, the reduction of vision to the immediate moment, was favourably received in 1929 because the essential aspects of the war which it conveys correspond quite closely to the surviving European folk-memory of trench warfare. In other words, *Im Westen* was the Great War *comme il faut*.

The structure makes few demands; it is an episodic series of anecdotes typifying the experience of the war generation as Remarque sees it: from school to basic training; the first taste of the front with a working party; the retreat to the rear; the front line again in all its horrors; the comic relief behind the lines when the hero and friends make their conquest of some local ladies; going on leave; the return to the front; being wounded, convalescent, and sent back to the fighting again; the increasing despair, apathy and perverse pride of the veteran, etc. Remarque knows how to emphasize by selection: we learn surprisingly little in detail about life in the trenches.[3] As Pfeiler pointed out, 'in a book which claims to be a report of the front by a front soldier, of 288 pages of text only about 80 pages deal with situations at or right behind the front, and even they are heavily interspersed with reflections' (p. 142). Strong emphasis is therefore thrown on to those aspects of the front which are mentioned, and from a documentary point of view certain exciting elements of 1914–18 warfare are dramatized unduly. There is the apparent frequency of the attacks (when much of front-line life consisted in reality of tedious and uncomfortable inactivity,[4] with the occasional patrol into no-man's-land or raid on enemy lines); there is hand-to-hand combat and the sight of the enemy dying slowly at your hands, in contrast to the dealing of death at long distance which was much more typical of the war.[5] There are the fits of berserk blood-lust that descend upon the attacker during an offensive.[6] None of the war-books avoids horrors, but Remarque heaps them up unmercifully (see the catalogue on p. 137). He is given to sensational touches and macabre effects to intensify the horrors of war: the screaming of the wounded horses (p. 66) is a sentimental and gruesome motif that became a feature of many a war-novel after *Im Westen* (see Bostock, p. 20). The first full-length description of action sets the scene in a churchyard where the hero cowers beneath a heavy artillery bombardment combined with a gas attack, while coffins fly through the air around him (p. 72). The elimination of each member of the small group of comrades by turn, until only the hero is left, is a conventional but effective technique, and the death of Bäumer at the eleventh hour, in the last days of October 1918, after he has survived the worst years of the war, is a somewhat sensational and contrived, though not impossible, dénouement.[7]. . .

. . . For officers on both sides, relief from the irons was much easier to achieve than for other ranks (although, of course, the casualty rate among officers was much higher). It is not surprising then to find that in the British books the hero still has to some degree a sense of being master of his own fate.[8] The same holds true for Jünger in *In Stahlgewittern* (for example, p. 75). But the sharpness of this contrast signifies more than a mere discussion of rank: it reminds us that *Im Westen* is a novel of Weimar Germany. Commentators have noted that in the last years of Weimar the individual became fully aware of his limited freedom of action in the face of social, industrial and political forces. Egon Schwarz sees the expression of this loss of identity as the chief function of *Neue Sachlichkeit* literature, namely 'das Augenmerk auf jene gigantischen und doch im Verborgenen wirkenden Kräfte zu richten, denen gegenüber die Bewegungsfreiheit des Einzelnen zu einer *quantité négligeable* zusammengeschrumpft war'.[9] The war in its later phase, the *Materialschlacht*, is highly symbolic of the mass industrial age voraciously devouring men and materials in a self-perpetuating system.[10]

In *Im Westen* this statement is always implicit, however, never enshrined in formal political utterances which might deter the reader. The characters of *Im Westen*, like so many created by the pacifist wing of *Neue Sachlichkeit*, are apolitical. The novel presents a very generalized pacifism, not a detailed programme but something akin to a pious wish for international amity, unlikely to arouse much resistance. Even then, the pacifism is diluted (certainly when compared to *Le Feu*!). After spending a night of profound penitence pinned down in a shell crater with the body of the Frenchman he has killed in hand-to-hand combat, Bäumer makes the dead man a promise he knows even at the time he cannot keep. . . .

. . . These thoughts, like a reversion to prayer in moments of danger, can be dismissed when 'normal' conditions are resumed.

Bäumer is kind to the Russian prisoners of war in his charge, and at one point his thoughts dwell on the process by which international treaties artificially create hostility between private citizens of different nations who bear each other no personal grudge (p. 194). But the front line is no place for such thoughts and they are banished to the margin for the duration: 'hier darf ich nicht weiterdenken. Dieser Weg geht in den Abgrund'. No doubt the implication is that the 1929 reader should be taking up this cause. Such pacifism seems today utterly banal.[11] The emotional appeal is simple and commits no one to action or the sacrifice of his personal interests. It even exists comfortably alongside the thrill of battle, the pride of the veteran soldier, and the assertion of Germany's undefeated military efficiency 'wir sind nicht geschlagen, denn wir sind als Soldaten besser und erfahrener' (p. 280). For many Germans in 1929, this must have offered a very acceptable package to fill (however momentarily) the moral vacuum experienced by the Weimar generation.[12] The message is delivered with a fervency which contrasts with its innocuous content: . . .

. . . The very modesty of Remarque's pacifism, such as it is, is highly appropriate to the nature of Weimar society, which, for all its cultural and artistic ferment, had in the main few ambitions in the direction of radical reform, and sought security rather than political revolution.

Notes

1. J. P. Stern, *Hitler: The Führer and The People* (London. 1975), p. 26.
2. See *Im Westen nichts Neues*, first edition (Berlin, 1929), pp. 266–7. All subsequent page references are to this edition.
3. Compare other war-books: Graves, Blunden, or Jünger (e.g. pp. 56–8 of *In Stahlgewittern*). We also learn very little from Remarque about the sufferings of the alien civilian population, a lack which is surprising in a supposedly pacifist novel whose hero is based for three years on occupied territory. Once again, it forms a contrast to Jünger's *In Stahlgewittern*, where there is frequent and sympathetic mention of the French civilians (e.g. pp. 190, 221). See also Arnold Zweig's *Erziehung vor Verdun* (1935; new edition, Berlin and Weimar, 1974), p. 76.
4. Compare Jünger, *In Stahlgewittern*: 'Statt der erhofften Gefahren hatten wir Schmutz, Arbeit und schlaflose Nächte vorgefunden, deren Bezwingung ein uns wenig liegendes Heldentum erforderte. Schlimmer noch war die Langeweile, die für den Soldaten entnervender als die Nähe des Todes ist' (p. 19). See also p. 189: 'Wieder machte ich die Erfahrung, daß kein Artilleriefeuer die Widerstandskraft so gründlich zu brechen vermag wit Nässe und Kälte.'
5. See C. E. Montague, *Rough Justice* (London, 1926): 'not many men died by the bayonet, in the whole of the war' (p. 340), and his *Disenchantment* (London, 1922), p. 157. Also Aldington's *Death of a Hero*, (London, 1929), p. 292: 'The fighting was so impersonal that

it seemed rather a conflict with the dreadful hostile forces of Nature than with other men . . . Actual hand-to-hand fighting occurred, but it was comparatively rare. It was a war of missiles, murderous and soul-shaking explosives, not a war of hand-weapons'.

6. Compare *In Stahlgewittern*, where Jünger reports of an attack: 'Der ungeheure Vernichtungswille . . . verdichtete sich in den Gehirnen und tauchte sich in rote Nebel ein' (p. 250). If this phenomenon was known on the British side, it has left very little record in the war-books, though we certainly find the same fighting fury in Barbusse's novel *Le Feu*. C. E. Montague specifically takes Barbusse to task for what he calls the 'doctrinaire fire' which makes the Frenchman pervert and exaggerate the 'thrill of drastic passion' (*Disenchantment*, p. 52). This response is typical of British writers' reaction to Barbusse's 'lack of restraint'! For Montague, the offensive is usually characterized by bathos, confusion, muddle, and 'the queer flashes of revelation, in contact with individual enemies, of the bottomless falsity of the cheaper kind of current war psychology' (p. 53).

7. Aldington's novel ends on the same note: in the very last days of the war, the hero practically throws his life away.

8. Officers were frequently seconded from the front for special courses of instruction: see Edmund Blunden, *Undertones of War* (London 1928), p. 251: 'It was wonderful to be promised an exeat from war for weeks, but I . . . felt as usual the injustice of my own temporary escape . . .'. Blunden is eventually blessed with six months' duty at a training centre in England, which effectively takes him out of the war altogether. Sherston in *Memoirs of an Infantry Officer*, recovering from a wound in the protective hospitality of Nutwood Manor, has the choice of taking an army job in England rather than returning to the front for the third time. Graves is offered a similar choice: 'In December I attended a medical board . . . The president wanted to know whether I wanted a few months more home service' (*Goodbye to All That* (London 1929), p. 293).

9. See *Die sogenannten zwanziger Jahre*, edited by Reinhold Grimm and Jost Hermand (Bad Homburg, 1970), p. 139.

10. That the war can be seen in quite a different light is demonstrated by Ernst Jünger, who stresses the scope for individualism granted to an officer in wartime: 'Eines den Vorrechte des Führers liegt darin, daß er in dieser Zeit den Massenbewegung allein gehen darf' (*Das Wäldchen 125*, in *Werke, Tagebücher* I, p. 371). Much closer to Remarque's tone is Arnold Zweig's version of war as an expression of the industrial society continued by other means: 'Die Infanteristen hier . . . sahen aus wie die abgetriebenen Herden dess Todes, Fabrikarbeiter den Zerstörung; sie batten alle die Gleichgültigkeit, die Industrie und Maschine dem Menschen aufpressen' (*Erziehung vor Verdun*, p. 174).

11. Yet we should bear in mind the violent response of many Germans to this harmless message at the time of the novel's appearance. 12. The sense of a vacuum manifested itself particularly in the search for a myth (in the broadest sense) by which to live: see the use of the term 'leerstehende Struktur' to express the post-war receptivity to myth in Germany, in Theodor Ziolkowski's essay 'Der Hunger nach dem Mythos', in *Die sogenannten zwanziger Jahre*, p. 198; and compare the term 'Leerformel' in Hans Schuhmacher's 'Mythisierende Tendenzen in der Literatur 1918–1933'. in *Die deutsche Literatur in der Weimarer Republik*, p. 286.

CHRIS DALEY ON THE FORCE OF SILENCE IN *ALL QUIET ON THE WESTERN FRONT*

Limits of Language

It is an obvious observation that where violence is inflicted on man it is also inflicted on language.

—Primo Levi

. . . As *All Quiet on the Western Front*'s narrator Paul Bäumer explains, "The attack does not come, but the bombardment continues. We are gradually benumbed. Hardly a man speaks. We cannot make ourselves understood."[7] The force of silence is demonstrated through the benumbing of the body; even the organs, limbs, and skin have failed to speak. More often than not, silence—the silence of guilt, shame, memories of unspeakable terror, or the corpse—becomes the transmission of emotion or the symbol of the futility of articulation.

In Remarque's novel, Paul Bäumer's frustrations with language as he tries to express the horrible and tragic nature of trench warfare make the reader more aware of how little can be understood without actual bodily participation. Remarque's novel is indeed a war story, but Bäumer never lets the reader forget his limitations in capturing the narrative "essence" of war. According to Bäumer, a war story cannot be properly written during war, or possibly even after, because the writer is not able to achieve tranquil objectivity or even sufficient

strength of rational analysis to assume the authority necessary to vouch for authenticity, to accurately witness. There is a reason why all is quiet on the western front and elsewhere. . . .
. . . Remarque also gestures toward silence's relation to dehumanization. We are unable to see what might become of Bäumer, because he finishes his narrative as yet another casualty, but we do see the fear, remorse, and guilt that accompany the one hand-to-hand killing he commits. Symbolically he stabs to death in a shell hole an enemy soldier who turns out to be a French printer, a distributor of language and possibly of the propaganda that had led them to the crater in the first place. Bäumer initially vows to write to the dead man's wife but reconsiders when he recalls the futility of words to express anything that happens in war. He realizes that language provides security from the truth; when he is required to console his dead comrade Kemmerich's mother back in Germany, he recognizes he would have to "invent a story" of Kemmerich's death and almost believe it himself (181). Language is distant and unreal; only war has presence: "Life is simply one continual watch against the menace of death;—it has transformed us into unthinking animals in order to give us the weapon of instinct— it has reinforced us with dullness, so that we do not go to pieces before the horror, which would overwhelm us if we had clear, conscious thought" (273–74).

This lack of clear, conscious thought adds an element of necessary fiction to any war narrative that claims authenticity. Even with conscious thought restored, an accurate narrative could not be written after the war, because the writer is restricted to language to express the events that have robbed him of expression and left him with silence. . . .

Limits of Morality
A thinking man's true answer to the question whether he is a nihilist would probably be "Not enough."
—Theodor W. Adorno

As far back as Horace, we have been informed that a piece of writing should entertain, but more importantly that it should instruct. According to Sir Philip Sidney, "This purifying of wit, this enriching of memory, enabling of judgement, and enlarging of conceit, which commonly we call learning, under what name soever it come forth, or to what immediate end soever it be directed, the final end is to lead and draw us to as high a perfection as our degenerate souls, made worse by their clayey lodgings, can be capable of."[8]

The moral of the story should lead us to higher virtue and enlightenment. Ideally, a narrative of war or atrocity would effectively persuade us to do whatever we could to prevent such an event from ever occurring again. Yet we are not that naïve. We have just ended a century that has produced a plethora of wars, war narratives, and still more wars, and we have just embarked on a century that promises much more of the same. Stories of war and atrocity do not serve as prophylactics. Besides, a narrative with a simplistic moral would not approach the "truth" needed to engage the reader in the first place. . . .

Even as *All Quiet*'s Bäumer narrates his story, he reinforces how futile verbal communication is when the horrors of war are beyond words: "How senseless is everything that can ever be written, done, or thought, when such things are possible. It must all be lies and of no account when the culture of a thousand years could not prevent this stream of blood being poured out, these torture chambers in their hundreds of thousands. A hospital alone shows what war is" (263). A hospital alone shows what war is because only its collection of bodies carries the true meaning of war, which cannot be expressed through rhetorical plaints or casualty lists. The materiality of blood and pain cannot be replaced by the pedantic attempts at cultural enlightenment through empty masterstrokes.

An important element in Bäumer's disillusion with language is his conclusion that language, in some ways, is directly responsible for the war.[9] As he discusses the reasoning behind the war with his comrades, he places the blame on the propaganda produced on both sides:

We didn't want the war, the others say the same thing— and yet half the world is in it all the same.

"But there are more lies told by the other side than by us," say I; "just think of those pamphlets the prisoners have on them, where it says that we eat Belgian children. The fellows who write those lies ought to go out and hang themselves. They are the real culprits." (206)

The separation is apparent between those making the war with language and those fighting the war with their bodies, those who design propaganda and those who stand accused of eating children. Bäumer correctly identifies the gulf between his generation, who die daily in the trenches, and the previous generation, who create ideologies and implements of war: "I see how peoples are set against one another, and in silence, unknowingly, foolishly, obediently, innocently slay one another. I see that the keenest brains of the world invent weapons and words to make it yet more refined and enduring. . . . What will happen afterward? And what shall come out of us?" (263–64). Words thus become synonymous with weapons as tools of destruction even as they also demonstrate their inability to function as tools of expression. The question as to what will happen afterward is the clamor for a moral, any moral, to provide a rationale for the relentless massacre of soldiers on both sides of the Great War, and to allow this story to be told.

Notes
7. Erich Maria Remarque, *All Quiet on the Western Front* (New York: Ballantine, 1928, repr. 1982), 107.
8. Sir Philip Sidney, "An Apology for Poetry" in *The Critical Tradition*, ed. David H. Richter, 2d ed. (Boston, Mass.: Bedford, 1998), 139.
9. Dawes's disciplinary model—see note 2 here.

HILDEGARD EMMEL ON *ALL QUIET ON THE WESTERN FRONT* AS A WEIMAR NOVEL

Independent of the new century's great experiments in novelistic form a body of literature evolved during the Weimar Republic which was produced by many talented authors and was rich in thematic and topical variations. The authors were committed to social criticism and ideological goals and saw that their needs were best met by the traditional, chronologically structured narrative. Just as Goethe's novels continued to have an effect throughout the nineteenth century—although contemporary modes of thought had long since prevailed—twentieth-century novelists could choose between the experiments of their own age and the traditional forms from the previous century: the *Zeitroman*, the historical novel, and the *Gesellschaftsroman*. . . .

. . . This literary trend reached its climax in a series of impressive novels which appeared between 1925 and 1932. Some of them achieved worldwide success, were printed in large editions, and were translated into many languages. Yet today only a few are still known to the German-speaking public. As values, literary tastes, and political realities changed over a half century, many of the once famous works underwent a radical devaluation, and others still remain controversial. A listing of the most famous titles will not entirely reveal the diversity and breadth of this literature which encompasses social, nationalistic, and religious themes as well as statements of political engagement, confessions of faith, and analyses of the times. Nevertheless the names of representative novels will serve to define boundaries and provide points of reference: *Jew Süss* (Lion Feuchtwanger), *The Devil* (Alfred Neumann), *A Nation without Space* (Hans Grimm), *The Case of Sergeant Grischa* (Arnold Zweig), *The Veil of Veronica* (Gertrud von le Fort), *Class Reunion* (Franz Werfel), *The Maurizius Case* (Jakob Wassermann), *Revolt of the Fishermen of Santa Barbara* (Anna Seghers), *Berlin Alexanderplatz* (Alfred Döblin), *All Quiet on the Western Front* (Erich Maria Remarque), *Success* (Lion Feuchtwanger), *The Wish Child* (Ina Seidel), *Little Man—What Now?* (Hans Fallada), and *Radetzky March* (Joseph Roth). The list could easily be lengthened since these authors were prolific writers whose activity spanned several decades.

These authors' involvement with current events stems from the emotional experience of the First World War and its aftermath. In the nineteenth century, attempts to develop the *Zeitroman* were seldom successful; authors found little inspiration in their own times, and, burdened by the oppressive weight of a great tradition, they felt dependent upon its themes and motifs. Their relation to their own times was founded more on theoretical considerations than on strong feelings rooted in contemporary events. By contrast, the First World War, the Revolution of 1918, and the postwar chaos had made the transforming effect of historical events on people and society so obvious that authors could not resist giving literary form to such overwhelming occurrences. A neutral, distanced manner of presentation was out of the question; the author's personal involvement determined his view of the epoch.

The books that deal with the experience of war demonstrate this with particular clarity. As unassumingly as Erich Maria Remarque (pseudonym of Erich Paul Remark, 1898–1970) narrates *All Quiet on the Western Front* (*Im Westen Nichts Neues*, 1929), he nonetheless shows emphatically how man is changed by war. It is a twofold process: on the one hand, human nature is laid bare, and on the other, the soldiers accept the realities honestly and openly. The willingness to acknowledge facts that were previously concealed or denied is characteristic of the new man, for whom social conventions have become obsolete. Shocking situations, such as in the opening scene, exemplify this: after half the company has fallen at the front, the rest of the unit is glad to receive double rations of bean soup and tobacco. The young soldiers display their unabashed delight over the large portions. As survivors they have no option but to view their physical needs objectively and without shame and to help their comrades as long as they can still be helped. Only the present hour is important to them; the world of parents and educators had slipped away during the first barrage. Warfare contradicts the ideals with which they grew up, and they have no idea how they will ever be able to return to a life so totally disrupted by war.

Like the majority of war novels of its day, *All Quiet on the Western Front* has no particular plot. In diarylike, chronologically ordered sketches, Remarque presents incidents from the war experiences of a group of young soldiers who went to school together and volunteered for the army under pressure from a teacher. The book alternates between periods at the front and peaceful interludes, horrifying battles and scenes of young comrades passing time together, episodes in the field hospital and at home on furlough. When the soldiers occasionally discuss the problem of war, they do so with few words and without intellectual pretension; they are its victims and see no sense in it. They realize that their enemies, the French and the Russians, are, like themselves, entangled in something utterly foreign to them and are also suffering. In their eyes the real enemy is Himmelstoss, the drill sergeant who bullies the recruits. The company commander, Bertinck, is regarded as a magnificent front-line officer. The novel's main character is the forty-year-old reservist, Katczinsky, an experienced and unselfish man who stands by the others. After his death all that remains to be reported is the death of the narrator. The last of seven in his class, he falls on a day so uneventful that the military report simply states: "All quiet on the western front." The narrator functions as the spokesman for the youths who, as a group, represent an army of millions of simple soldiers. As characters they do not differ substantially from each other, nor is the narrator particularly distinguished from the rest. It is a generation which, according to the author's preface, was destroyed by the war, including those who managed to escape its shells. The narrator argues along the same lines, claiming that on the front soldiers become "human animals." But these assertions are contradicted by the altogether humane behavior of the soldiers in all situations, which would seem to suggest hope for the future. The book was a worldwide success, sold millions of copies (probably six to eight million), and was translated into approximately thirty languages. Remarque was influenced by Henri Barbusse's (1873–1935) *Le Feu—Journal d'une escouade* (1916), a war novel published while the war was still being fought. . . .

. . . In summary, the ideological literature of the Weimar Republic may serve as a model example of a literature which had practically no effect despite the authors' best intentions to change their society. The novels found many readers, but they had little influence on the political development of the country from which their material, ideas, themes, and inspiration were derived. The ideologies advocated by and in the novels either could not be implemented at all, or; if they were implemented, then it was by men who most certainly did not develop their views from novels. The authors' opposition to war, their pleas for social justice, and their analyses of historical or contemporary events cannot be shown to have influenced public opinion. On the contrary, the ideas which came to prevail found few proponents among novelists during the Weimar Republic. Therefore, after the collapse of the Republic, the majority of known and respected German novelists were forced into emigration.

Vita Fortunati on the Representation of World War I in Hemingway, Remarque, and Ford Madox Ford

Comparing three novelists as different as Ford, Remarque and Hemingway is not an easy task. The working hypothesis of my essay is that although Ford, Remarque and Hemingway came from different cultures and backgrounds, and even if they were of different ages when they underwent this terrible experience, the war narratives they produced all show that the traditional historical novel form was in a profound state of crisis, as suggested by the great critic György Lukács.[1] These three writers were all clearly aware that the war could no longer be narrated in a traditional way because what they had witnessed was a historical event that broke with the past completely. The First World War not only called into question the very notion of 'History' as a story dominated by the principle of causality, it also made epic narrative impossible as the useless sacrifice of millions of young men at the front was so blatantly senseless. In these novels rhetoric is out of the question and what takes its place is a pervasive sense of death and desolation. The characters in these novels are aware that they are the victims of a system that has created a situation whose logic and meaning they can no longer grasp. . . .

. . . Both Hemingway's and Remarque's novels were written after their war experiences. Remarque was very young, only seventeen, when he was called up in 1917. He fought at the front in Northwest France, at Verdun, the stage for the 'battle of Flanders', one of the most atrocious battles of the First World War. *All Quiet on the Western Front* is commonly defined as a 'confession novel'. It was published in 1929, more than ten years after the war had finished. Hemingway's novel, *A Farewell to Arms*, a fictionalised rendering of his experiences in Italy as a Red Cross ambulance volunteer, was also published in 1929. Both works are based on personal experience and both mix autobiographical events with fiction. The works insist on the role of their authors as witnesses and it is no coincidence that Remarque's epigraph echoes this feeling: 'this book is intended neither as an accusation, nor as a confession, but simply as an attempt to give an account of a generation that was destroyed by the war—even those of it who survived the shelling'. They are two tragic witness accounts by what was later to be defined as the 'lost generation' or the 'battlefront generation', a generation that could not and would not forget the faults of those who had created such a senseless war. Both Hemingway and Remarque wrote more than once of the sins of the fathers.[12] There is an unmistakable spirit of rebellion against the false teachers who had sung the praises of the war, and used their triumphantly romantic and idealistic rhetoric to push young people like themselves into such a tragic 'adventure':

We often tried to find a reason or an explanation for this, but we can never quite manage it. Things are particularly confused for us twenty-year-olds, for Kropp, Muller, Leer, and me, the ones Kantorek [our teacher] called young men of iron. The older men, still have firm ties to their earlier lives—they have property, wives, children, jobs and interests, and these bonds are all so strong that the war can't break them. . . . We hadn't had a chance to put down any roots. The war swept us away. (*AQWF* 14)

Hemingway and Remarque's generation marched off to war with their heads full of abstract concepts such as 'honour' and 'glory'. They left with the idea that they were the saviours of democracy, the saviours of the fatherland but these ideals soon crumbled in the face of the stupidity and irrationality of unbending military discipline and the brutal conditions that the common soldier had to bear in the trenches.[13] It is from this bitter observation that Remarque's strong anti-military sentiments grew: Remarque's novel was even censored for being defeatist not only because of its ferocious criticisms of the military system, but also for its desolate vision of a generation that had lost everything and who would always bear the wounds of a trauma that could never be cured. The idea of the war as a marking experience that would always deprive its victim of happiness is a painful leitmotiv in Remarque's novels: 'If we had come back in 1916 we could have unleashed a storm out of the pain and intensity of our experiences. If we go back now we shall be weary, broken-down, burnt-out, rootless and devoid of hope, we shall no longer be able to cope' (*AQWF* 206).

The main character in *A Farewell to Arms* also brings back deep moral and physical wounds from the war. In the general confusion following the disastrous retreat from Caporetto he is unjustly accused of being a deserter; so, shocked and disillusioned, he decides to settle what he calls a 'separate peace'. This is the formula that Hemingway uses to express the sentiments of an entire generation who had had enough and who were rebelling against an unjust society without, however, having any drive really to reform it: '. . . I had the paper, but I did not read it, because I did not want to read about the war. I was going to forget the war: I had made a 'separate peace'. I felt damned lonely and was glad when the train got to Stresa.'[14]

In both novels any rhetorical attitude towards the war is rejected and the two authors strive to reconstruct the story of what happened as objectively as possible. Remarque's novel is a series of sketches, a collection of journalistic accounts where dialogues provide the structure for the whole story. Therefore the scenes stand as separate tableaux, and the only thing that holds them together is the voice of the main character remembering his painful experiences at the front. Remarque's fragmentary structure perfectly suits the sense of discontinuity and lack of cohesion characterising this new form of war narrative, where historical interpretation has been replaced by the agonised testimony of someone who has lived through an experience which is still very hard to tell. The tone of Remarque's novels oscillates between that of a journalist's reportage and the intimate jottings of a diarist. Time in a historical sense has disappeared altogether and instead we are thrown into a subjective sense of time, as the narrator waits anxiously in the trenches. There he lives in a present that seems to have no end and silent images crowd into his head as the shells explode deafeningly around him.

Both Hemingway and Remarque develop a style that is 'lean', bare, concise and essential; a style that seeks to convey the sense of precariousness that pervades life at the front. Both novels are also characterized by their use of irony and paradox, by their sense of grotesque and expressionist exaggeration, especially in the descriptions of the terrible mutilation of bodies; a grotesqueness which is emphasised by their consistent use of understatement. The final ironic phrase of Remarque's novel, where the author's voice impassively announces the death of the narrator, offers an emblematic example: 'He fell in October 1918, on a day that was so still and quiet along the entire front line that the army despatches restricted themselves to the single sentence: that there was nothing new to report on the western front' (*AQWF* 207).

Similarly, Ford's tetralogy, as Samuel Hynes has rightly pointed out,[15] is not only a book about the First World War, as his aim was to record the profound change that this apocalyptic event had had on a whole era. And yet, his claim that, like Proust, he wanted to be the social historian of his age had to reckon with his lucid awareness of having serious difficulties in describing the war. Ford knew perfectly well that the First World War represented a new type of war which also put into question the old war narrative. In addition, Ford, in his poetics, emphasized, that anyone who attempted to recount a historical event, inevitably ended up interpreting it and creating a narrative which blurs 'facts' and 'fiction'. This new epistemological stance needs innovative narrative techniques, which Ford drew from avant-garde experiments. Exploring the experimental works of post-impressionist painters, such as Italian futurists, vorticists, and cubists, as well as literary and musical avant-gardes, Ford struggled to create new forces, which like that of the futurist poetry, succeeded in using onomatopoeia to suggest the deafening explosions of mortar shells and the other new weapons. Similarly, from a visual point of view, he also used stains of colour to depict the brown mud of the battlefields and the red blood of the dead bodies.

Notes

1. György Lukács, *Der historische Roman*, Neuwied und Berlin: Luchterhand, 1965.

12. See for the relationship between 'Parents-and-Children' during pre-war and post-war period, the provocative pamphlet by Wyndham Lewis, *The Old Gang and the New Gang*, New York: Haskell House Publisher, 1933. In this essay, Lewis criticises Remarque's 'sentimentalism' and his 'morbid and hysterical' mood (p. 52). Lewis's position is rather ambiguous, since on the one hand he insists on saying that we 'are all a Lost Generation', and on the other hand, he criticises Eliot's 'Hollow men' mentality. In this essay, in fact. even if he criticises younger generation's feeling about war, he nevertheless expresses his own war rhetoric of 'not capitulate entirely'. Similarly, for Lewis, 'although modern War is wholly devoid of glory, the glory of the human spirit is indestructible' (p.58).

13. Mario Isnenghi, *Il mito della Grande Guerra*, Bologna: il Mulino, 2002; see in particular Chapter 4. 'La Truppa'.

14. Ernest Hemingway, *A Farewell to Arms*, London: Penguin, 1963—henceforth *FA*; p. 188.

15. Samuel Hynes, *A War Imagined*, New York: Atheneum, 1991.

Dorothy B. Jones on the Film Version of the Novel

Death and darkness are ever present in *All Quiet on the Western Front*. Our first view of the war front is a small village on a dark day. The streets are full of mud; there is a confusion of men, mounted troops, and hospital trains, while exploding shells in the distance throw up dirt and debris; night comes on, and a pouring rain makes the scene even more dismal. The boys' first assignment to action is to lay barbed wire just beyond a graveyard at night. Here the first death of their group occurs. The big battle is fought in a dull and desolate light which is neither day nor night. In a later sequence, a graveyard serves as the place of battle; and Paul, digging frantically to secure himself from enemy fire, is horrified to find that he has dug himself into a coffin and is lying beside a corpse. Toward the close of the film, as the men march into battle on the eve of the great offensive, they joke grimly about the coffins piled up by the roadside.

In contrast to the depressing darkness, raw brutality, suffering, and death of the war scenes, *All Quiet on the Western Front* gives us in other scenes glimpses of sunlight, untroubled youth, love, and the joy of living. Early in the film, the freshness, fun, and eagerness of youth are fully expressed in the picture of Paul and his comrades. In the classroom, although they are wide-eyed and earnest, they are also full of gay and noisy enthusiasm; in the barracks, before Himmelstoss makes his appearance, they are exuberant, obviously proud of themselves. This same untroubled youthfulness—this time in counterpoint to the dull, darkened spirit of Paul who has returned from the front—is again seen in the classroom toward the close of the film.

But youth and a love of life in contrast to death are most strikingly dramatized in a brief scene after the death of Franz Kemmerich. Paul, holding Franz's boots in his hand, stands shocked and grief-stricken at the top of the steps leading from the terrace of the hospital. For a moment he remains motionless, quietly absorbed by his inner feelings; then, his features begin to relax. From a deathlike mask of grief his face comes to life before our eyes, expressing deep relief and the joy of being alive, as he descends the stairs and begins to walk, slowly at first (the camera traveling with him), then faster, faster (past the camera), his mood and step growing lighter until he is running swiftly down the pathway through a little wood (away from the camera). The sun is shining on the path, and several young soldiers strolling toward the hospital call to him as he runs past them. "What's your hurry?" one asks, adding to his companion half-jokingly, "I bet he stole those boots." They both laugh and look after him, as the picture fades from view. This brief scene captures perfectly the feeling experienced by almost every soldier at the death of a comrade. After the first shock there immediately follows the natural relief felt by the survivor, a poignant sense of joy at finding himself alive. He cannot help feeling glad that someone else, even though a friend, rather than he has died; and suddenly he becomes acutely aware of his own aliveness, infused as he is with relief and joy and a sense of his own well-being. So Paul, running down the sunlit path, running away from death, expresses this intense, deeply felt urge to live. And the boys who call out to him, by their secure air of normalcy, by their very casualness, heighten our understanding of the intensity and the meaning of Paul's behavior. Unfortunately, Lewis Milestone followed this scene by another in which Paul, returning to his quarters, tells Muller how he felt after Franz's death. Coming directly after the scene just described, Paul's speech is merely a verbal repetition of an idea which has already had eloquent cinematic expression.

All Quiet on the Western Front tells us that even during wartime, people of the warring nations, taken as individuals, can have feelings of love and compassion for one another. This idea is expressed in two scenes which are among the most effective in the entire film. Paul has found shelter in a shell hole when a French soldier descends upon him. Paul stabs his enemy with his bayonet. Finding himself alone with the groaning Frenchman, Paul tries to escape, but the fighting is still too heavy overhead. Horrified, he sees that his hands are covered with blood, and he tries to wash off the blood in the water hole at the bottom of the crater. Now it is night, and we hear the Frenchman groaning in the dark. The flash of exploding shells now and again lights up the crater to reveal the Frenchman lying against the side of the hole and Paul hunched over, his hands covering his ears to shut out the man's agonized moans. The morning light finds Paul disheveled and frantic.

He tries to get the Frenchman to drink and realizes that he is dead. With his half-smiling lips and staring eyes, he appears to look accusingly at Paul.

This is one of the scenes of the film which Lew Ayres, in his first important screen role as Paul, is not quite able to handle convincingly.[1] Nevertheless, its effectiveness is felt because of the powerful truths which are expressed as the German youth speaks to the Frenchman he has killed. War demands that men kill one another. But a man can feel compassion for another human being, regardless of his nationality. Face to face with the Frenchman whom he has mortally wounded, Paul is overcome by pity and remorse. From "the enemy," whom he has been taught by the necessities of war to fear, hate, and kill, this Frenchman becomes simply another human being, a man like himself, for whom Paul feels great compassion. In a small crater in the midst of the battle, Paul is overcome by these emotions, and we know that each man who kills so ruthlessly on the battlefield is essentially capable of these same emotions.

Love between the children of the warring nations is also expressed in a tender love scene between Paul and a French girl. Paul, Albert, and Leer pay a night visit to three French girls across the river, bringing them bread and wine. They sit with the girls around a table and watch them eat and drink. Later, from a close-up of a victrola turning unheeded at the end of a record, the camera draws back to take in the quiet, deserted room. Then a bedroom is shadowed on the wall. We see only the shadows of the head of the bedstead and a water pitcher on the table, as we overhear Paul and Suzanne talking quietly together. Paul speaks to her gratefully; but Suzanne, who cannot understand his words, interrupts him repeatedly with a whispered "Poor boy—this terrible war!" We know that in the arms of this girl the youth has found momentary escape from war; whereas, the French girl, in giving her love, grieves at what has happened to this German boy, just as millions of women—mothers and wives the world over—grieve over what war does to their men.

Here with taste and simplicity has been recorded one of the most eloquent love scenes ever filmed. The motionless shadows on the wall are expressive of the quiet mood of the lovers. At the same time since we cannot see them we listen the more intently. Yet, the words which this boy and girl speak are unimportant. The gentle tone, the tenderness in their voices are what matter; although they speak in different tongues, their language is a universal one. The effectiveness of this scene stems in part from its appeal on a primary level of experience: like children, we listen outside a forbidden door; and, like children, we hear not so much the words as the tone. What we hear are the universal intonations of love as a boy and girl of the warring nations express their love for one another.

Note
1. Lew Ayres was only twenty years old when he played the part of Paul in this film. It was not until some years later in the middle 'thirties, when he traveled extensively in Europe, that his convictions as a pacifist were definitely formulated. However, he states that his first big screen role in *All Quiet on the Western Front* made a tremendous impression upon him and was undoubtedly an important factor in determining his attitude toward war. When called into service in World War II, Lew Ayres declared himself a conscientious objector and was interned. However, he agreed to serve in the U.S. Army Medical Corps and in this service distinguished himself on battlefields in the South Pacific.

HELMUT LIEDLOFF ON *A FAREWELL TO ARMS* AND *ALL QUIET ON THE WESTERN FRONT*

Hemingway's *A Farewell to Arms*[1] and Remarque's *Im Westen nichts Neues*[2] are two of the few books about World War I which are still read today, which have the reputation of being classics in this field. In the case of *Farewell* it would be belabouring the obvious to prove the general critical acclaim. In the case of *Im Westen* the case appears to be less clear. To some post–World-War-Two critics it is "only" a report, journalistically written, not of sufficient depth, in short, not serious literature.[3]. . .
. . . The similarity of the topics invites a critical comparison of the two novels in regard to symbolism, language, structure,

development of character, the extent of the depiction of war, and the attitude of the authors towards war. It should be pointed out, though, that Hemingway has engaged the attention of critics much more than Remarque. This circumstance heavily influences the emphasis on Remarque in this paper.

Right in the beginning of the two novels, one of the main differences between them becomes obvious. Many critics have noted that the opening of *Farewell* expresses in its symbolism almost the entire story: the clearness, the dryness, the leaves falling early that year, the richness of the crops, and, finally, the rain. These symbols appear again and again throughout the novel, e.g. the rain as a leitmotif suggesting death. There is little doubt that *Farewell* makes extensive use of symbolism, whereas *Im Westen* employs comparatively little. Some instances in the latter, however, appear as a definite attempt in this direction. For instance, when Paul comes home from the front, he finds that his suit fits no more (page 166), suggesting that he outgrew his past and everything he left when he became a soldier. Among other things, he left his butterfly collection, which is mentioned twice (pages 160 and 162). Taken together with the fluttering butterflies which rest on the teeth of the skull before the front trench (page 130) they might be understood as suggesting the world of beauty that Paul has to leave behind. The movie made use of the butterfly in this sense at the very end: on a quiet day, when Paul is in the front trench, a butterfly flutters near him. Paul forgets for a minute his by then almost instinctive cautiousness, reaches for the butterfly and is hit at that very moment by a sniper's bullet. His latent yearning for the world of beauty is finally fatal. Paul's last name is suggestive of this yearning for beauty, as the name Bäumer brings to mind both "Baum" (tree) and "Träumer" (dreamer), two terms which have considerable significance for Paul's character. Tree suggests organic growth, the idea of wholeness—things Paul is yearning for or dreaming of. Some other names also have a suggestive quality. Thus the name Haie Westhus has a regional form and points to Haie's close relation to his moor, while the name of Katcinsky, which has in it the word for "cat", points in another direction. As the head of the group, he is "zäh, schlau, gerissen, . . . und [mit] einer wunderbaren Witterung für dicke Luft, gutes Essen und schöne Druckposten" (page 9), all qualities which make us think of the instinct of an animal. In a later paragraph the importance of the animal image will be discussed.

Although the importance of symbolism in *Farewell* is obvious, a comparative analysis of both novels suggests that it should not be carried too far, either. One critic, for instance, by applying too rigid a symbolic framework, sees the Rinaldi of after the "bad summer" as a man without resources, without God, as a man of the plain[4]. This interpretation disregards other details of the story, e.g., that Rinaldi belongs to the group, that he is a close friend of Frederic, and that his partial breakdown occurs after the "bad summer" precisely because he is very much aware of what is going on, because he is "realizing" the war. Remarque is much more explicit on the topic of the breakdown than Hemingway. . . .

. . . This case of "Frontkoller," as Remarque calls it, reminds one very much of that of Rinaldi after the "bad summer." He unreasonably attacks the priest:

"To hell with you, priest!" . . . "To hell with you," said Rinaldi. "To hell with the whole damn business." He sat back in his chair . . . "I don't give a damn," Rinaldi said to the table. "To hell with the whole business." He looked defiantly around the table, his eyes flat, his face pale. (pages 184–185)

Remarque records two other cases of seasoned soldiers suddenly breaking down: Detering, who deserts and is caught shortly thereafter and shot (pages 270–271), and Berger, who forgets his usually instinctive caution to take care of a wounded dog and gets fatally hurt (page 273). To speak of these men as being "without resources," to put them into one category with the unaware, the incompetent, does not seem justified.

Through the same emphasis on the supposedly basic symbolic structure of the novel, the figure of the priest and the cold, clear mountain world are made the antithesis of the filthy, godless plain where the war is fought[5]. However, fighting and rain do occur in the mountains, too, and the love story does take place in Milan, a city of the plain[6]. Interestingly enough, also in *Im Westen* there appears a series of paragraphs describing a much-longed-for, wholesome world. . . . The beauty and wholesomeness of this "other" world is recognized in either case. But both Bäumer and Lt. Henry realize that they are not part of it. This becomes particularly clear if one carefully reads the description of the Abbruzzi by the priest; it is not a real possibility for Henry—it is an idyll, and so is the life with Catherine in the Alps above Montreux idyllic. Reality, the war, death, the rain will catch up with them.

Parallel to the greater importance of symbols in Hemingway is the greater restraint in his language. His adjectives and verbs are strictly descriptive, with very little directly emotional value. For instance the scene at the bridge where Lt. Henry is arrested: nowhere is there any of his feeling given, everything is transposed into situation and action:

> The other one grabbed me from behind and pulled my arm up so that it twisted in the socket. I turned with him and the other one grabbed me around the neck. I kicked his shins and got my left knee into his groin. (page 238)

Another good example is Frederic's farewell from Catherine in Milan or the closing paragraph of the novel. The detachment, which is not necessarily an inner one, is stressed by the frequent use of the "there are" phrase and such words as "nice, lovely, fine" etc. These worn-out words with almost no precise meaning at all contribute to the low-key atmosphere of the whole.

Although both novels are told in the first person—how different is Remarque's language. Colloquialisms occur not only in the dialogue as in *Farewell* but also in the narrative itself. It is full of soldier-language expressions: ". . . ein Kochgeschirr voll [Essen] fassen; sich hinhauen; dicke Brocken; Gulaschmarie." (pages 7–8)—In other instances the language becomes, particularly in the beginning, colloquial; for instance: "Er bietet das Essen *direkt* an; er weiss nicht, wie er seine Gulaschkanone *leerkriegen* soll (page 7); sie würden einen *schönen* Schrekken *kriegen.*" (page 130)—Such expressions are proper in the actual conversation but bothersome in the narrative because they disrupt its unity. In other parts it is difficult to decide whether the language is inadequate or whether it is the substance as such that is insufficient. There are numerous passages, particularly in the beginning of the novel, where the narrator thinks about the situation he has just told.

Notes

1. Ernest Hemingway, *A Farewell to Arms* (New York: The Modern Library, 1932). All quotations in this paper are from this edition; the page numbers are given in parentheses in the text.

2. Erich Maria Remarque, *Im Westen nichts Neues* (Berlin, 1929). All quotation in this paper are from this edition; the page numbers are given in parentheses in the text.

3. See Heinrich Spiero, *Geschichte des deutschen Romans* (Berlin, 1950), pp. 559, 561; see also Albert Soergel and Curt Hohoff, *Dichtung und Dichter der Zeit* (Düsseldorf, 1963), II, 345, 349; Fritz Martini, *Deutsche Literaturgeschichte*, 8th ed. (Stuttgart, 1957), p. 559.

4. Carlos Baker, "The Mountain and the Plain," *Ernest Hemingway: Critiques of Four Major Novels*, ed. Carlos Baker (New York, 1962), p. 54.

5. See Carlos Bayer, *op. cit.*, particularly, pp. 51–55.

6. E. M. Halliday, "Hemingway's Ambiguity: Symbolism and Irony," *Ernest Hemingway: Critiques of Four Major Novels*, ed. Carlos Baker (New York, 1962), p. 68.

ALFREDO BONADEO ON PAUL BÄUMER'S RELATIONSHIP TO GERMAN CULTURE

Degradation is not exclusive to one country or one society. It knows no national boundaries; it only knows personal value and sensibility. The paths it follows vary and its representation differs from writer to writer; but its presence is discernible in all countries at war. Had Paul Bäumer, the protagonist of *All Quiet on the Western Front*, lived, he would have found it impossible, not just hard, like T. E. Lawrence, to go back to civilian life. The young German is part of a culture that welcomed war as the destroyer of a "world peace" that crawled with "spiritual vermin as with worms," fermenting and stinking of the "decaying matter of civilization," and as the triumph of German virtues—"fidelity, patriotism, readiness to die for an idea."[72] But Bäumer is at the periphery of that culture and he only bends to its dictates. Kantorek, his high school teacher, and the community which regards any young man lukewarm about fighting as a "coward," prod Bäumer, and he joins up. As a dutiful German soldier he plays the role that his fatherland assigns to him. He, like his comrades in the novel, "loved" his country and "went courageously into every action." The reality of the war, however, impresses him more than the moral imperative exalts him, and he quickly learns that if "duty to one's country is the greatest thing . . . death-throes are stronger."[73] As a result of his background and attitude Bäumer's deterioration is different than Lawrence's. The German does not, like the legendary guerrilla, subtly reflect on the ways war changes him; instead his simple but quick mind, unsupported by stirring patriotism, tells him that at the front the soldier that changes into an animal has a better chance of survival than the soldier who does not adjust. But Bäumer will also discover that if animality saves his skin—at least for a time—over the years it diminishes him as a man. Since animality allows him to survive, it is a virtue, but since it robs him of his humanity, animality is also a poison that destroys him. The contrast between the struggle to survive physically and the loss of Bäumer's humanity brought about by that struggle creates the tension that pervades Remarque's novel.

The novelist points at the young soldiers' already sunken state at the beginning of his novel when, after returning from the front line, he describes them as "satisfied and at peace." But their satisfaction does not come from having gained a victory or a medal; it comes from their having eaten well: "Now our bellies are full of beef and haricot beans. . . . Each man has another mess-tin full for the evening; and, what is more, there is double ration of sausage and bread." The satisfaction of physical needs is of special importance to the soldiers; it is the ideal and exploit they value the most and it is also a substitute for the inner strength needed to live a life which is a living death: "But our comrades are dead, we cannot help them, they have their rest—and who knows what is waiting us? We will make ourselves comfortable and sleep, and eat as much as we can stuff into our bellies and drink and smoke so that the hours are not wasted. Life is short."[74] In a world where human values are crumbling, relief from fear and loss comes from those things that satisfy man and animal alike.

At the front, Bäumer and his comrades transformed themselves quickly into lower beings because the army had prepared them well for the change. During military training they saw that authority kills the best in man: intelligence, education, and culture. "We learned," Bäumer recalls, "that a bright button is weightier than four volumes of Schopoenhauer. . . . We recognized that what matters is not the mind but the boot brush, not intelligence but the system, not freedom but drill." He also learned that the authority of a mere corporal has influenced him more than his parents, teachers, and "the whole gamut of culture from Plato to Goethe." Bäumer discovers early what T. E. Lawrence found out at the end of the war—that submission to military discipline is "renunciation of personality such as one would not have asked of the meanest servant."[75] The training, however, gives the soldier an instrument for survival in the form of toughness and animality: "We became hard," Bäumer recognizes, "suspicious, pitiless, vicious, tough. . . . Had we gone into the trenches without this period of training most of us would certainly have gone mad. We did not break down but endured. . . . By the animal instinct that is awakened in us we are led and protected." This instinct tells the soldier when and where to run, when to duck and to hit the ground when bullets and bombs fly. It assumes control of the soldier as soon as he faces the enemy; and the soldier consigns himself willingly to the instinct because his survival depends on it; "We march up, moody or good-tempered soldiers—we reach the zone where the front begins and become on the instant human animals. . . . We turn into animals . . . because this is the only thing which brings us through safely. . . . We want to live at any price."[76]

In *All Quiet on the Western Front*, "the front is a cage" in more than one sense. It both holds men doomed to idleness and bloody fighting, and it houses animals. Under a French infantry attack preceded by a vicious bombardment, Bäumer and his comrades retreat while they fire and fling hand grenades; Remarque's description of the scene skillfully blends dehumanization ("thugs, murderers"), animality ("cats") and struggle for survival: "We have become wild beasts. We do not fight, we defend ourselves against annihilation. . . . No longer do we lie helpless, waiting on the scaffold, we can destroy and kill, to save ourselves. . . . crouching like cats we run on, overwhelmed by this wave that bears us along, that fills us with ferocity, turning us into thugs, into murderers; . . . this wave that multiplies our strength with fear and madness and greed of life, seeking and fighting for nothing but our deliverance." These soldiers fight fiercely but are not heroic; Remarque does not even call them soldiers; he calls them "men," precisely "dead men." But they are very much alive, for their bodies, impelled by the animal, move vigorously; what is dead in these men is their soul. And, as in some other tales of battles, when the fighting dies down, the soldiers temporarily regain their humanity, Bäumer and his comrades "gradually . . . become something like men again." They become only something like men, not quite men, for as soon as they complete the retreat their thoughts turn to food ("the corned beef over there is famous along the whole front . . . we have a constant hunger") to the satisfaction of animal needs. They secure jam, cognac, turnips, five tins of corned beef, a thin loaf of white bread, and settle down for a big meal. In the eating scene Remarque blends the fulfilling of physical needs with that of the highest purpose of the animal, survival: "It is a good thing we have something decent to eat at last; we still have a use for all our strength. Enough to eat is just as valuable as a good dug-out; it can save our lives; that is the reason we are so greedy for it."[77]

The transformation into a lower being dejected T. E. Lawrence, but ostensibly does not bother Bäumer, because he believes that animal toughness will save him—physically. In a way he justifies his transformation into beast. Life at the front, he says of his group, "has transformed us into unthinking animals in order to give us the weapon of instinct . . . it has lent us the indifference of wild creatures." But Bäumer is also aware of the change's sinister meaning: the soldiers have become wild through a perversion of existence's purpose; while in life man strives to improve himself, in war he struggles to debase himself: "Our inner forces are not exerted toward regeneration, but toward degeneration. The Bushmen are primitive and naturally so, but we are primitive in an artificial sense, and by virtue of the utmost effort." The soldiers' deliberate perversion heightens the consciousness of their depravity and opens the door to a potential crisis ("unexpectedly a flame of grievous and terrible yearning flares up"); and to the protagonist of *All Quiet on the Western Front* the crisis finally comes when he realizes that he is no longer human. Like Lawrence, Bäumer is first split into two selves, one set up against the other in a dialogue without any understanding: "In the quiet hours when the puzzling reflection of former days, like a blurred mirror, projects beyond me the figure of my present existence, I often sit over against myself, as before a stranger, and wonder how the unnameable active principle that calls itself life has adapted itself even to this form." Life adapted itself to killing, and has degraded. Then Bäumer realizes that he no longer belongs to humanity. As he knows that he is incapable of regaining his human self after an action ("we turn into animals when we go up to the line . . . so we turn into wags and loafers when we are out resting. We can do nothing else, it is sheer necessity"), so he knows that he could not return to normal living even if he were to survive the war.

Notes

72. Thomas Mann in 1915, quoted by Fritz Stern, *The Politics of Despair* (Berkeley, 1961), p. 206; Ernst Glaeser, *Class of 1902*, trans. W. and E. Muir (New York, 1929), pp. 206–7.

73. Remarque, *All Quiet on the Western Front*, pp. 18, 20.

74. Ibid., pp. 7, 155. The novel places unusual stress on food and related bodily functions; for instance; "The soldier is on friendlier terms than other men with his stomach and intestines. Three quarters of his vocabulary is derived from these regions, and they give an intimate flavour to expressions of his deepest indignation" (p. 15). On

this aspect see C. Barker and R. Last, *Erich Maria Remarque* (London, 1979), pp. 50, 56.

75. Remarque, *All Quiet on the Western Front*, pp. 29–90.
76. Ibid., pp. 35, 65–66, 154–55.
77. Ibid., pp. 126–127, 129, 131–32.

MODRIS EKSTEINS ON THE NOVEL AS A POSTWAR COMMENTARY

Remarque stated the purpose of *All Quiet* in a brief and forceful prefatory comment:

> This book is to be neither an accusation nor a confession, and least of all an adventure . . . It will try simply to tell of a generation of men who, even though they may have escaped its shells, were destroyed by the war.[9]

The story then recounts the experiences of Paul Bäumer and his schoolmates, who move from the classroom to the trenches, bursting with energy and conviction, enthusiastic knights of a personal and national cause. One by one they are ripped apart at the front, not only by enemy fire but also by a growing sense of futility. The war is transformed from a cause into an inexorable, insatiable Moloch. The soldiers have no escape from the routinized slaughter; they are condemned men. They die screaming but unheard; they die resigned but in vain. The world beyond the guns does not know them; it cannot know them. "I believe we are lost," says Paul.

Only the fraternity of death remains, the comradeship of the fated. At the end Paul dies, forlorn yet strangely at peace with his destiny. Peace has become possible only in death. The final scene of the American film version of the novel was to be a masterly evocation, of the mood of Remarque's work: a sniper's bullet finds its mark as Paul is reaching from the trench to touch what the war had rendered untouchable, a butterfly. All the shibboleths lose their meaning as the men die violent deaths—patriotism, national duty, honor, glory, heroism, valor. The external world consists only of brutality, hypocrisy, illusion. Even the intimate bonds to family have been sundered. Man remains alone, without a foothold in the real world.

The simplicity and power of the theme—war as a demeaning and wholly destructive, indeed nihilistic, force—are made starkly effective by a style that is basic, even brutal. Brief scenes and short crisp sentences, in the first person and in the present tense, create an inescapable and gripping immediacy. There is no delicacy. The language is frequently rough, the images often gruesome. The novel has a consistency of style and purpose that Remarque's earlier work had lacked and that little of his subsequent work would achieve.

Despite Remarque's introductory comment and his reiteration of the point in later statements, very few contemporary reviewers noted, and later critics have generally ignored, that *All Quiet* was not a book about the events of the war—it was not a memoir, much less a diary[10]—but an angry declaration about the effects of the war on the young generation that lived through it. Scenes, incidents, and images were chosen to illustrate how the war had destroyed the ties, psychological, moral, and real, between the generation at the front and society at home. "If we go back," says Paul, "we will be weary, broken, burnt out, rootless, and without hope. We will not be able to find our way any more." The war, Remarque was asserting in 1928, had shattered the possibility of pursuing what society would consider a normal existence.

Hence, *All Quiet* is more a comment on the postwar mind, on the postwar view of the war, than an attempt to reconstruct the reality of the trench experience. In fact that reality is distorted, as many critics insisted—though with little effect on the initial acclaim for the novel. Remarque's critics said that at the very least he misrepresented the physical reality of the war: a man with his legs or his head blown off could not continue to run, they protested vehemently, referring to two of the images Remarque had used. But far more serious than such shoddiness, they claimed, was his lack of understanding of the moral aspects of soldiers' behavior. Soldiers were not robots, devoid of a sense of purpose. They were sustained by a broad spectrum of firmly established values.[11]

Although his publisher did not like such admissions, because they undermined the credibility of the novel, Remarque was prepared to say that his book was primarily about the postwar generation. In an exchange in 1929 with General Sir Ian Hamilton, the British commander at Gallipoli in 1915 and now head of the British Legion, Remarque expressed his "amazement" and "admiration" that Hamilton for one had understood his intentions in writing *All Quiet*:

> I merely wanted to awaken understanding for a generation that more than all others has found it difficult to make its way back from four years of death, struggle, and terror, to the peaceful fields of work and progress.[12]

It was, in part the misinterpretation of his purpose that led Remarque to write a sequel to *All Quiet*. *Der Weg zurück* (*The Road Back*), a novel published in 1931, explicitly argued the case of the "lost generation."

All Quiet can be seen not as an explanation but as a symptom of the confusion and disorientation of the postwar world, particularly of the generation that reached maturity during the war. The novel was an emotional condemnation, an assertion of instinct, a *cri d'angoisse* from a malcontent, a man who could not find his niche in society. That the war contributed enormously to the shiftlessness of much of the postwar generation is undeniable; that the war was the root cause of this social derangement is at least debatable; but Remarque never took part in the debate directly. For Remarque the war had become a vehicle of escape. Remarque and his book were, to borrow from Karl Kraus, symptoms of the disease they claimed to diagnose.

Notwithstanding Remarque's opening declaration of impartiality—that his book was "neither an "accusation nor a confession"—it was in fact both. And it was more. It was a confession of personal despair, but it was also an indignant denunciation of an insensate social and political order, inevitably of that order which had produced the horror and destruction of the war but particularly of the one that could not settle the war and deal with the aspirations of veterans. Through characters identifiable with the state—the schoolmaster with his unalterable fantasies about patriotism and valor, the former postman who functions like an unfeeling robot in his new role as drill sergeant, the hospital orderlies and doctors who deal not with human suffering, only bodies— Remarque accused. He accused a mechanistic civilization of destroying humane values, of negating charity, love, humor, beauty, and individuality. Yet Remarque offered no alternatives. The characters of his *generazione bruciata*—the Italian notion of a "burned generation" is apt—do not act; they are merely victims. Of all the war books of the late twenties—the novels of Arnold Zweig, Renn, R. H. Mottram, H. M. Tomlinson, Richard Aldington, Hemingway, and the memoirs of Graves, Blunden, Sassoon, to name but a few of the more important works—Remarque's made its point, that his was a truly lost generation, most directly and emotionally, even stridently, and this directness and passion lay at the heart of its popular appeal.

But there was more. The "romantic agony" was a wild cry of revolt and despair—and a cry of exhilaration. In perversion there could be pleasure. In darkness, light. The relation of Remarque and his generation to death and destruction is not as straightforward as it appears. In his personal life and in his reflections on the war Remarque seemed fascinated by death. All of his subsequent work exudes this fascination. As one critic put it later, Remarque "probably made more out of death than the most fashionable undertakers."[13] Like the Dadaists, he was spellbound by war and its horror, by the act of destruction, to the point where death becomes not the antithesis of life but the ultimate expression of life, where death becomes a creative force, a source of art and vitality. A young Michel Tournier, on meeting Remarque, noted the paradoxical nature of this modern author-hero: world famous for his antimilitarism, Remarque, "with his stiff posture, his severe and rectangular face, and his inseparable monocle," looked like a larger-than-life Prussian officer.[14]

Many of Remarque's generation shared his apocalyptic post-Christian vision of life, peace, and happiness in death. George Antheil would, when appearing in concert to play his own music, carry a pistol in his evening jacket. As he sat down to play, he would take out the pistol and place it on the piano. The .25 caliber Belgian revolver that Harry Crosby used in December 1929 to kill himself and his mistress had a sun symbol engraved on its side. A year earlier, while saluting Dido, Cleopatra, Socrates, Modigliani, and Van Gogh among others, he had promised soon "to enjoy an orgasm with the sombre Slave-Girl of Death, in order to be reborn." He yearned to "explode . . . into the frenzied fury of the Sun, into the madness of the Sun into the hot gold arms and hot gold eyes of the Goddess of the Sun!"[15]

Notes

9. *Berliner Börsen-Zeitung,* June 9, 1929; *New York Times,* November 17, 19:9; *Daily Herald,* November 12, 1929.

10. *The Cambridge Review,* May 3, 1929, 412.

11. *The London Mercury,* 21 (January 1930), 194–95.

12. Reported in the *New York Times,* February 9, 1930.

13. H. A. L. Fisher, *A History of Europe,* 3 vols. (London, 1935), I: vii.

14. "War Novels," *Morning Post,* April 8, 1930.

15. André Thérive, "Les Livres," *Le Temps,* December 27, 1929.

HANS WAGENER ON THE FINAL CHAPTER OF *ALL QUIET ON THE WESTERN FRONT*

Looking closely at this description of what lost youth represents, we find that on the one hand it is a yearning for things romantic, for something still to be found in books and thus not real but ideal; on the other hand it constitutes unrealistic expectations with regard to the future, a kind of fulfillment to be derived from a relationship with a woman, presupposing a romantic picture of women which is just as unrealistic. Remarque deplores the loss of innocence that he finds in youth, just as many other writers envision children as symbols for innocence. Clinging to such visions would mean clinging to illusions. To be sure, Remarque makes the aspect of inner destruction more profound by not giving his protagonist the ability to develop more specific ideas about the future and instead having him escape from reality into childhood dreams. On the other hand, we might argue that according to his own biography Remarque himself did not have any more precise ideas. We might also argue that it is not natural for this kind of dreaming to be cut short by the horrors of war. The natural growing process should have been allowed to be more gradual and kinder. However, it is logically just as unjustified to make the war responsible for a necessary maturing process. In his next novel Remarque was to say that education has a similarly negative effect on people. This opinion stems from a romantic notion of what man is supposed to be, a pathetic denial of the necessity of growing up, of adjusting to the realities of adulthood.

In the final two short paragraphs of the book a new narrator is introduced who reports Bäumer's death in a few words. Bäumer was killed in October 1918, on a day that was so quiet on the entire front line that the report in the daily war bulletin was reduced to a single sentence: "All quiet on the Western front." The irony is, of course, that if Bäumer was killed, it was not all quiet on the western front. Thus, Remarque stresses the impersonal character of the killing, the discrepancy between a military point of view and the actual suffering and dying of millions of soldiers, of individual human beings. The title of the book itself thus becomes an accusation, and the entire novel refutes the callous statement of its title: it is not true that it was all quiet on the western front (the literal translation of the German text is "nothing new in the west"). It is incidentally not true that Remarque used a standard phrase of the German army high command. But he did choose a phrase that summarized the cold exigencies of the military value system. This is, also incidentally, the first time in the book that a precise date is given, by reference to the historical daily war bulletin. By taking the change of seasons into consideration, it is possible thus to conclude that the action took place roughly between the summer of 1917 and October 1918.

Remarque does not reveal the identity of the new narrator who gives a seemingly objective report and thus creates a distance between Bäumer and the reader. Yet he does describe the expression on Bäumer's face when he was turned over—a tranquil expression of being almost satisfied that it turned out that way, which makes us believe that this narrator is really one of Bäumer's comrades.

Since the entire preceding narration was first-person narrative, and since Bäumer nowhere in his story explicitly implies that he is writing a diary, this conclusion of the novel does not logically follow from the lost-generation theme. Although Bäumer's death was foreshadowed in numerous ways, it occurs in contrast to the theme of the lost generation, that is, those soldiers, who had escaped the physical destruction of war and remained consequently lost in the society. Thus, the initial statement of the novel can not refer to Bäumer but only to Remarque himself who made himself a spokesperson for the majority of his intended readers, former soldiers of World War I. Given Remarque's tremendous success as a writer, it seems almost ironic that this success is based on the prediction that war destroyed the generation he writes about and made it impossible for them to succeed in real life.

As is obvious from the above quotations, Remarque has tried to write in a simple nonliterary language.[4] He is trying to imitate the normal spoken language of the German front-line soldier with all its repetitive formulas and filler expressions that often say very little, its drastic slang, metaphors and comparisons that often derive their crude humor from references to digestive bodily functions. He thus writes in a style that is the opposite of the Neo-romantic style he used in *Die Traumbude*; indeed, he consciously avoided the somewhat stilted and sophisticated language of literature and used expressions that at the time were considered not acceptable for a literary work of art. The fact that the text is replete with soldiers' jargon identifies the narrator as a simple soldier who speaks the language of the majority of the front-line soldiers. This language, which was so familiar to the majority of the novel's readers, comes across as honest because it does not have the ring of "literature." Remarque thus wants to create the impression that a simple soldier and not a professional writer is giving a truthful report about the war. Through his language the narrator clearly appears as the mouthpiece of millions of soldiers.

This realistic language, however, is often interrupted by soft, lyrical passages which are emotionally charged and which at the same time are reminiscent of the "old," Neo-romantic Remarque of *Die Traumbude* and his early poetry. The following passage may serve as an example:

> The parachute-lights shoot upwards—and I see a picture, a summer evening, I am in the cathedral cloister and look at the tall rose trees that bloom in the middle of the little cloister garden where the monks lie buried. Around the walls are the stone carvings of the Stations of the Cross. No one is there. A great quietness rules in this blossoming quadrangle, the sun lies warm on the heavy grey stones, I place my hand upon them and feel the warmth. At the right-hand corner the green cathedral spire ascends into the pale blue sky of the evening. Between the glowing columns of the cloister is the cool darkness that only churches have, and I stand there and wonder whether, when I am twenty, I shall have experienced the bewildering emotions of love (*AQ* 119).

The images conjured up in this passage are in stark contrast to the war environment which surrounds Bäumer at that time. At other times, however, similar imagery even serves to romanticize scenes of war. In the above passage it is designed to idealize the memories of early youth and peace in order to underscore the loss of youth brought about by the horrors of war. One might be tempted to criticize Remarque for shifting from one stylistic mode into another, but passages such as the above can easily be explained by attributing them to the former student Bäumer, who had literary ambitions and who was taken directly out of school to be trained as a murderer. Bäumer's education has not endowed him with the ability to rationally question the origin or purpose of war; it is rather the reason for his heightened sensibility.

Notes
4. In the following discussion of style and structure I am largely following the analysis of Rüter, 74ff.

ROBERT BAIRD ON HOLLYWOOD'S AMBIVALENCE TO WORLD WAR I NOVELS

Critical Scene #2: No Man's Land

All Quiet, a more consistently artful and fully integrated work than *Angels*, has its own spectacular scene of large-scale warfare. Although the great bulk of injuries and deaths in *All Quiet* are staged as prosaic and nonstrategic, the middle section of *All Quiet* portrays a massive British assault and German counterassault, following a grueling five-day bombardment. Forced to deal with spectacle (the historical reality of war's size and fury) and the possibility of exciting a film audience with scenes of large-scale battle, director Lewis Milestone uses a number of alienating strategies to undercut his own action sequences. His first and most consistent strategy is to undermine, through staging and editing, the strategic omniscience of a viewer. Unlike the battle scenes of the war romance, where a clear cause-and-effect chain of attack, retreat, action, and reaction will be intertwined with the principal characters, Milestone evokes the chaos of battle by overwhelming the frame with teeming soldiers and incessant shelling, by rapid editing, and by rapid presentation of the action. In other words, unlike the romantic battle scene, which coherently stages principal characters amid a chaotic background of combat, *All Quiet* loses its principal characters amid battle confusion. Denying the viewer a strategic visual perspective (bird's-eye-view, for example) or strategic verbal description (officers' commentary) of a battle restricts the film's narration to the foot soldier's view. The soldier "extras" are also presented in such a way that any personal cause and effect sequence is undermined. By this I mean that Milestone often cuts away from action as it is occurring, where a war romance might often isolate individual combatants and their actions amidst the confusion of battle.

A second alienating strategy used by Milestone is one of the most noted formal effects of *All Quiet*—the famous machine-gun pans, tracking shots taken from behind machine-gun positions as the weapon sweeps down rows of attacking infantrymen. The power of this formal presentation of combat is comparable to that of *Angels'* zeppelin suicides, for here, too, a filmmaker has joined camera movement, staging, and narrative to create a visual expression of World War I combat that evokes a powerful intuitive response. Milestone joins the clackety mechanization of cinema (camera/projector) to the mechanization of the machine gun, the success of mechanical camera panning/projecting ironically critiquing the ease of machine-gun panning—a horrible harmony of form with content. Further, the speed of the tracking camera/machine gun, and that the victims are passed over before they are given time to fall, reflects back on the nonstrategic staging of the entire battle. The shift in worldview is from the God who notices a sparrow's fall to the camera/machine gun that does not dally on a dying soldier's fall. Milestone further undercuts the possibility that the first "machine-gun tracking shot" against the attacking British troops can be read as the prowess of German soldiery and technology (the taking of sides that most war romances indulge in); he does this brilliantly by giving the British defenders the same "machine-gun" tracking shot, but reversed, now right to left, as the Germans counterattack. With such a (camera) move, Milestone visually and formally marks World War I ground combat as a mechanized and impersonal mass murder.

Milestone's last alienating effect is a bit of shock editing worthy of the Grand Guignol. In an image lasting only an instant, a British soldier lunges into the German barbed wire just as a shell detonates near him. Horrifically, the soldier's hands are left dangling, grasping the barbed wire the soldier never scaled. Such an image serves as a literal expression of mechanized, meaningless death, for such a death resists transcendental and personal meaning. The apparent instant dematerialization of nearly an entire body violates one's innate image of the whole body, obliterates any conception of heroism, and haunts the mind long after its perception.

The terrible balance of *All Quiet*'s one action sequence between attack and counterattack reflects the historical failure of World War I military strategy to anticipate or break the 360-mile-long snake of trenches that for four years lay across Europe. By denying Kat, Paul, and their fellows a clearly arranged and individualized position through the confusion of battle, Milestone dramatically challenges Hollywood's traditional reliance on evolving action and strategic agency in the war romance.

The different presentations of the zeppelin sequence and the *All Quiet* infantry battle, one staged strategically and one nonstrategically, offer enough contrast to justify the distinction between war romance and realist war film. However, the elements these two scenes share serve to limit any pure categorization of either film as romantic or realist, strategic or nonstrategic, myth-maker or demythicizer. Indeed, Milestone's attempt to delineate a simple relationship to war spectacle must be seen in light of the ongoing development of film sound in 1930 Hollywood. Robert Sklar raises a point against the typical belief that *All Quiet*'s success was founded solely in its antispectacular realism:

> At its most basic level, sound was noise, and noise itself could be a source of thrills. Hollywood did not tear down its boudoir sets overnight, but the possibilities of sound attracted filmmakers more and more to noisy settings. War was one, and Lewis Milestone's *All Quiet on the Western Front* became the big hit of 1930. Two world-war air spectacles—Howard Hughes's *Hell's Angels* and Howard Hawks's *The Dawn Patrol*—were also popular that year. (176)

This emphasis on sound is apparent in *All Quiet's* sound track, in particular the five-day bombing of the trenches and the infantry battle. The sound here is not only impressive (the density and distortion of the blasts), but also the sheer relentless repetition of blasts is remarkable. Also of note is the force of the sound of shelling to literally obliterate dialogue and other diegetic sound, a cinematic attempt to approximate the deafening potential of real shelling. In its sound, then, *All Quiet* is as spectacular as the air spectacles. This element provides support for the observation that it is impossible to film war without glorifying it through its inherent spectacles. If the air picture is disparaged for its emphasis on spectacle in general, and sonic spectacle in particular (recall that *Wings* was presented theatrically with a crude film sound system that triggered plane-like diving and roaring sounds from behind the screen, and that Hughes literally remade *Hell's Angels* in order to add the spectacle of sound to his film), then what critical stance is to be taken toward a lauded example of antispectacle such as *All Quiet*, which, to some degree, successfully exploited the rapidly developing sound technologies of its day?

Death in Spectacle and Antispectacle

Another forceful contrast is highlighted when the deaths of the central protagonists of *All Quiet* and *Hell's Angels* are analyzed side by side. Kat Katczinsky (played brilliantly by character actor Louis Wolheim) is a bullish, almost indestructible old veteran who shelters Paul and his young student volunteers as best he can. Near the end of the film, Kat is literally badgered and bombed to death by a single biplane during a sunny walk that reunites the old veteran with Paul, just back from leave. The greatest separation of the romantic and realist vision of World War I can be seen in comparing Kat's death in *All Quiet* and *Hell's Angels'* single image (twenty-five seconds) of trench warfare. *All Quiet* represses and distorts the air war just as certainly as *Hell's Angels* represses and distorts the ground war. Milestone and Hughes repress World War I content, and when they do briefly acknowledge the existence of the second arena of combat, the dialectic, they do so with extremely pointed staging and for narrative contrivance.

Kat's death scene begins with the veteran out searching for food (he might as well be berry picking). Paul sees his old friend and they meet and embrace. Low on the soundtrack is the drone of a single airplane. Milestone uses three cutaways of medium long shots to present a distant airplane. The shots are so distant that the plane and its flyer remain impersonal, almost gnat-like. The plane drops one bomb and wounds Kat. Paul hoists his large friend onto his back and begins carrying him to an aid station. While Paul consoles his friend, the plane drops another bomb, which kills Kat, although Paul fails to notice his friend's fatal injury and that the larger-than-life Kat has shielded his young friend from death—as he has so many times before. Remarque's novel stages Kat's death in much the same way, but without the single plane—indeed, it is apparently artillery shelling that kills Kat in the novel; however, just before Kat's death, Remarque includes this passage: "There are so many airmen here, and they are so sure of themselves that they give chase to single individuals, just as though they were hares. For every one German plane there come at least five English and American. For one hungry, wretched German soldier come five of the enemy, fresh and fit" (247). Milestone successfully turns the romantic flyer into a distant, mechanical weapon, chasing and destroying Kat, the most impressive embodiment of human survival and strength in the entire film. This is to pose the airplane as machine against man, where the air picture poses man embracing machine. Milestone has a biplane destroy not only Kat but the rebonding and comradeship of Kat and Paul. In this way, the last symbol of World War I romance becomes the murderer of *All Quiet*'s only celebration: male (human) bonding in time of war.

Hughes's repression of trench warfare is even more extreme than *All Quiet*'s denial of the air. It is only until the very last scene of the film, after Monty and Roy have given their lives in order to save hundreds of 7th Brigade infantrymen, that Hughes shows thirty seconds of ground combat.

Wilhelm J. Schwarz on Remarque's Memorial to the Unknown Soldier

As Ernst Jünger's war diary could be considered a monument to the heroic leader, so *Im Westen nichts Neues* by Erich Maria Remarque might be called a memorial to the unknown soldier. Paul Bäumer, the hero of Remarque's book, also joins the armed forces as an eighteen-year-old volunteer. His teacher, Kantorek, delivers fervent patriotic speeches until the whole class of twenty students with idealistic and romantic views about life and war march to the *Bezirkskommando* to sign up. Only one student, Joseph Behm, a good-natured boy, wavers. The others finally persuade him to enlist also. Perhaps there are other boys who think as he does. But nobody can stand back at a time when even parents are inclined to use the word "coward."

Strange to say Joseph Behm is the first one to die in action. During an attack on the enemy lines he is shot in the eyes and abandoned for dead. In the afternoon he begins to call for help and crawls frantically around between the lines without sense of direction. Wild with excruciating pain and unable to see, he fails to take cover and is shot by the French before anybody can go to bring him in. Remarque raises the question of responsibility for the death of this boy, one of many who had to die before they began to live.

Im Westen nichts Neues opens the statement that the book is neither an accusation nor a creed but only an attempt to report on a generation of men who were destroyed by the war even though they may have escaped its grenades.[3] Yet this book is an accusation of the generation that preached that service to the state was the highest aim in life.

On the battlefield in Belgium and France, German youth is emancipated from the *Weltanschauung* of the older generation. Remarque states:

(While they were still writing and talking, we saw the wounded and the dying. While they called service to the state the greatest thing, we knew already that the fear of death is stronger. We did not become mutineers, deserters or cowards because of this—all these expressions were freely used by them—we loved our homeland as much as they and we went courageously into each attack. But now we differentiated. All of a sudden we had learned to see. And we saw that nothing of their world was left. We were suddenly terribly alone and alone we had to cope with it.)[4]

Jünger, of course, encounters no problem of this nature. At least there is no indication of it in his writings. He gladly accepts the whole system of German militarism from his sergeant to his Kaiser. He is a soldier and executes the orders of his superiors without questioning their authority Of high personal integrity, he does his duty conscientiously and punctiliously. He makes his whole existence unconditionally subservient to the need of his country. While being sent to Heidelberg for treatment of an injury he reflects: "Wie schon war doch das Land, wohl wert, dafür zu bluten and zu sterben."[5] (How beautiful the country was, well worth bleeding and dying for.) While recuperating from another wound in a military hospital, he gives the whole of his possessions, three thousand marks, to the state in the form of a *Krigesanleihe*, a war bond.

Apart from the above cited passage and the love of country it reflects there is scarcely any indication that Jünger is concerned with the causes of the war, its aim and justification, its legitimacy or its absurdity. Basically he sees in the war only an unparalleled chance for adventure, an opportunity to unleash all his hidden Viking instincts. . . .

****

Such ambitions, of course, are foreign to Paul Bäumer, or Remarque. Bäumer's enthusiasm for the army, for the war, for heroism and all types of military activity is crushed and squelched in the barracks, never to be revived again. One morning he has to make his bed fourteen times for Corporal Himmelstoss. He has to scrub the corporal's mess with a toothbrush. He has to remove the snow from the yard of the barracks with a handbrush and a dustpan. Sarcastically he states that he is becoming an unequalled master of *Kniebeugen*, of knee-bending. The life in the barracks, where a former mailman, now in the uniform of a corporal, is wielding almost unlimited power over a group of fear-ridden boys, breaks his idealism and all his illusions about the "great time." "Wir lernten, dass ein geputzter Knopf wichitiger is als vier Bände Schopenhauer.[7]... (We learned that a polished button is more important than four volumes of Schopenhauer.... We became soldiers with enthusiasm and good-will but they did everything to knock that out of us.) And yet, there comes a time when he almost yearningly looks back to this period of human degradation. This is the time of the great slaughters and massacres.

****

Women do not play any role in Jünger's war diaries. It is true that a French girl invites him for supper on one occasion. If any intimate relations develop he does not mention them, although he describes the meal with meticulous care: eggs, white bread and butter, lying very appetizingly on a cabbage leaf. In the town of Brancourt he is lodged with a French couple and their very pretty daughter. One day, quite accidentally, he encounters her when she is nude—to the embarrassment of both. But he shows no further interest in her. There is no indication that he has any relations, however harmless, with a girl in Germany. He is a warrior made of Krupp steel. In his spare time he reads, with great pleasure, the whole of Ariosto's writings.[15]

Paul Bäumer is not a warrior. He is simply a human creature. He has exchanged the world of his youth for this nightmare of hell upon earth:

(Drum-fire, barrage-fire, curtain-fire, mines, gas, tanks, machine-guns, hand-grenades—words, words, but they encompass the horror of the world. Our faces are scabby, our thinking is laid waste, we are dead-tired—when the attack comes, some need to be beaten with fists so that they will wake up and come along.)[16]

Year after year he listens to the whining of the shells and only sometimes—when he feels the air warmly and softly caressing his face—does he think about girls and blooming meadows and white clouds and about his irrevocably lost youth.

Paul stands with his friend, Albert, in front of a big poster giving notice about a troupe that is to visit the fighting units. Depicted in the poster is a girl in a bright summer dress and white shoes. "Es ist ein ganz herrliches Mädchen, mit einer schmalen Nase, mit roten Lippe und langen Beinen, unvorstellbar sauber und gepflegt, es badet gewiss zweimal am Tage und hat nie Dreck unter den Nägeln."[17] (She is an extremely beautiful girl, with a thin nose, red lips and long legs, unbelievably clean and well-groomed. She certainly bathes twice a day and never has dirt under her finger nails.) They find it hard to understand that this is a picture of a girl who really exists, a girl of flesh and blood.

And then he meets a French girl, a gentle, small, dark young woman who strokes his hair and says, "La guerre—grand Malheur—pauvres garçons." And he feels her lips and he closes his eyes and he tries to wipe it all out, the war and the horror and the vulgarity, tries to become young and happy again. And he hopes for a miracle, an escape from the world of mud, and blood, and gas, and brothels before which the soldiers stand in a long queue.[18]

****

Although in Remarque's writings we never find a canonization of the man of courage, he by no means denies the existence of bravery. Yet there is a fundamental difference between the kind of courage that Remarque observes and that seen by Jünger. First of all he describes the desperate heroism of soldiers who, like threatened animals, are not really fighting but are rather defending themselves against annihilation. Out of love and lust for life they kill, destroy, cause havoc among those who come running across the fields with rifles, hand grenades and flame-throwers in their hands. They become heroes not because of some nebulous ideal that a rapturous schoolmaster, in the security of a classroom, has planted in them. It is a matter of killing or being killed, or of destroying so that one may live. These are the rules of conduct for the day and the basis of heroism as Remarque sees it.

Secondly, he sees the pitiful bravery of the young recruits who, barely more than children, have come directly from school to the battlefield, with only a few weeks of military training.

Notes
3. Remarque, *Im Westen nichts Neues*, p. 5.
4. *Ibid*, pp. 18-19.
5. Jünger, p. 40.
7. *Ibid*, p. 27.
15. *Ibid*, p. 156.
16. Remarque, p. 136.
17. *Ibid*, p. 144.
18. *Ibid*, p. 150-153.

Works by Erich Maria Remarque

Die Traumbude: Ein Küunstlerroman (1920).

Im Westen nichts Neues (1929); translated by A.W. Wheen as *All Quiet on the Western Front* (1929).

Der Weg zurück (1931); translated by A.W. Wheen as *The Road Back* (1931).

Drei Kameraden (1937); translated by A.W. Wheen as *Three Comrades* (1937).

Liebe deinen Nächsten Roman (1941); translated by Denver Lindley as *Flotsam* (1941).

Arc de Triomphe: Roman (1946); translated by Denver Lindley and Walter Sorell as *Arch of Triumph* (1945).

Der Funke Leben (1952); translated by James Stern as *Spark of Life* (1952).

Zeit zu leben und Zeit zu sterben (1954); translated by Denver Lindley as *A Time to Love and a Time to Die* (1954).

Der schwarze Obelisk: Geschichte einer verspätelen Ju gend (1956); translated by Denver Lindley as *The Black Obelisk* (1957).

Die Letzte Station (1956); translated by Peter Stone as *Full Circle* (1973).

Der Himmel kennt kiene Günstlmge (1961); translated by Richard and Clara Winston as *Heaven Has No Favorites* (1961); translation republished as *Bobby Deerfield* (1961).

Die Nacht von Lissabon (1963); translated by Ralph Manheim as *The Night in Lisbon* (1964).

Schatten im Paradies (1971); translated by Ralph Manheim as *Shadows in Paradise* (1972).

Annotated Bibliography

Baird, Robert. *"Hell's Angels above the Western Front." Hollywood's World War I: Motion Picture Images* (1997): 79–100.

Discusses Hollywood's simultaneous production in 1930 of two opposing perspectives on the World War I battlefield by contrasting the novel, *Hell's Angels*, a book valorizing aviation and reveling in the spectacular, with *All Quiet on the Western Front*, an antiwar novel firmly rooted in a realistic representation of the horrors of combat. Baird provides an insightful analysis, noting important distinctions between these two vastly different novels on which these films are based and suggests that their divergent points of view may be due to the dissimilarity between warfare fought in the air as opposed to the reality on the ground. "Romantic spectacles like *Hell's Angels* celebrate the individual as causal agent of history generating Great Man narratives. Realist films such as *All Quiet on the Western Front* present individuals as the effects of history, objects buffeted by their environment."

Bance, A.F. *"'Im Westen Nichts Neues':* A Bestseller in Context." *The Modern Language Review*, vol. 72, no. 1 (January 1977): 359–373.

This work analyzes the success of *Im Westen nichts Neues* (*All Quiet on the Western Front*) as a work representative of the war experience of the Weimar Republic. Bance discusses the dramatic circumstances surrounding its initial publication in book form in January 1929 by the Ullstein publishing house, an event inaugurated by an unprecedented publicity campaign that led to its translation into fourteen languages within a mere few months, followed by its condemnation by the Nazis in December 1930, which only further added to its success. These dramatic events notwithstanding, Bance attributes Remarque's achievement to various formal elements that distinguish *All Quiet* from other novels about the war experience, namely his ability to present the combat experience in fictional form with a simple episodic structure in a seemingly ahistoric context. "*Im*

Westen nichts Neues comes close to being all things to all men. . . . The war was distant enough in 1929 to be discussed and thought about again; and yet it was not decent for it to be depicted without reservation as heroic and exemplary."

Bonadeo, Alfredo. "War and Degradation: Gleanings from the Literature of the Great War." *Comparative Literature Studies*, vol. 21, no. 4 (Winter 1984): 409–433.

Comparing *All Quiet on the Western Front* to other European novels about World War I, Bonadeo maintains that they share the same underlying theme of barbaric behavior that accompanies a loss of human identity, though their portrayals of the reentry into society differ. Bonadeo believes that if Paul Bäumer had managed to survive, he would utterly fail to be reintegrated into civilian life since he is the product of a culture that embraced war, though his commitment to the conflict is marginal. "As a dutiful German soldier he plays the role that his fatherland assigns to him. . . . But Bäumer will also discover that if animality saves his skin—at least for a time—over the years it diminishes him as a man."

"The Way Back: Alun Lewis and Remarque by Kathleen Devine." *Anglia*, vol. 103, no. 3 (1985): 320–335.

Comparing *All Quiet on the Western Front* with Alun Lewis's story "War-Wedding," Devine discusses the belief shared by these two works that the destructiveness of war renders impossible a meaningful return to the life left behind. For Lewis, an author who saw no action on the front and whose father was successful following his return from the war, Devine attributes his otherwise inexplicably grim perspective primarily to his reading of Remarque's novel. "No English writer in the inter-war period had expressed with such open emotionalism this tragedy of a lost generation, a tragedy that, as Remarque sees it, begins with the initial training which . . . require[s] of them a total 'renunciation of personality.'"

Eksteins, Modris. "Memory." *Rites of Spring: The Great War and the Birth of the Modern Age.* (1989): 275–299.

Emphasizing the importance of *All Quiet on the Western Front* as a commentary on the psychological aftermath of World War I rather than a representation of life in the trenches, Eksteins contends that Remarque's novel has been misinterpreted by critics who have judged its merits and weaknesses solely as a representation of "the physical reality of war." Eksteins states that *All Quiet* epitomizes the malaise of its postwar culture, while analyzing Remarque's life in the context of other artists of his generation as well as of public indifference during the Weimar years. "*All Quiet*, contrary to the claims of many of its enthusiastic readers, was not 'the truth about the war'; it was, first and foremost, the truth about Erich Maria Remarque in 1928. . . . The war boom of the late twenties reflected less a genuine interest in the war than a perplexed international self-commiseration."

Eksteins, Modris. "*All Quiet on the Western Front* and the Fate of War." *Journal of Contemporary History*, vol. 15, no. 2 (April 1980): 345–366.

Examining *All Quiet on the Western Front* as the focal point of a renewal of writings on World War I, Eksteins discusses the controversial debate sparked by Remarque's novel, not least of which was the question of the actual facts of the author's wartime experiences. Eksteins maintains that there was reason to suspect that Remarque's experience was not as extensive as those described by Paul Bäumer and, in fact, that Remarque's primary interest was in exploring the emotional consequences of his generation rather than reporting on the reality of trench warfare. This essay also provides an overview of early critical acclaim of the novel as well as a mounting opposition that began to form concurrently, including a pointed response from the extreme left that found *All Quiet* "an example of the sterility of bourgeois intelligence." Counterbalancing that position was a fascist outcry that the book "was pernicious because it threatened the entire meaning of postwar conservatism."

Emmel, Hildegard. "The Novel during the Weimar Republic." *History of the German Novel* (1984): 260–287.

Tracing the evolution of the novel as a vehicle for social criticism and ideological agendas, Emmel discusses a literary trend that flourished between 1925 and 1932 and produced many impressive works, which *All Quiet on the Western Front* ranks highly among. In his analysis of several of these novels, Emmel points out that although *All Quiet* is told in a straightforward, journalistic manner with little discussion among the soldiers, their true feelings about their horrifying situation can be understood by their behavior. "[T]he ideological literature of the Weimar Republic may serve as a model example of a literature which had practically no effect despite the authors' best intentions to change their society. . . . Therefore, after the collapse of the Republic, the majority of . . . respected German novelists were forced into emigration."

Firda, Richard Arthur. "Characters and Characterization." *All Quiet on the Western Front: Literary Analysis and Cultural Context* (1993): 52–61.

An expert on Remarque's work, Firda discusses the characterizations found in *All Quiet on the Western Front*, essentially three types of characters who either stand out or fade into the background much like the impressionistic painters of whom Remarque was so fond. Firda maintains that while pacifist sentiments are conveyed through the three-dimensional protagonist, Paul Bäumer, whose simple yet moving manner of speaking influences our acceptance of his credibility, intermediate characters such as Kat serve a more limited function, in this instance as a representative of the survival instinct, and background figures such as the Russian prisoners of war and the townspeople Bäumer meets while on leave. Firda further argues that these secondary and tertiary characters all refer back to and enhance Baumer's credibility. "Remarqe's background characters create the flotsam and jetsam of wartime humanity; without them, Bäumer's meditations on the futility of war would remain only abstract philosophical essays."

Firda, Richard Arthur. *"Post Mortem: All Quiet on the Western Front (1929)." Erich Maria Remarque: A Thematic Analysis of His Novels.* New York: Peter Lang Publishing, Inc. (1988): 29–64.

Discussing *All Quiet on the Western Front* in the context of Remarque's life, Firda places the novel within the social and political context of the Weimar government, beginning with his move to Berlin in 1925 and his subsequent editorial position at *Sport im Build.* Firda provides a close reading of the text that interprets the novel in terms of Remarque's wartime experiences and the circumstances surrounding its early publication, both in Germany and internationally, as well as providing an overview of the initial critical responses.

Fortunati, Vita. "The Impact of the First World War on Private Lives: A Comparison of European and American Writers (Ford, Hemingway, and Remarque)." *History and Representation in Ford Madox Ford's Writings* (2004): 53-64.

Comparing *A Farewell to Arms* to *All Quiet on the Western Front,* Fortunati states that both these novels, which are tragic eyewitness accounts of World War I by writers who are protesting the horribly misguided authority figures that urged participation in the war, are to be distinguished from Ford Madox Ford's four-volume work which reflects the author's understanding of World War I as something new that would require an innovative way to express the changes it contained and ushered in. This observation on Ford's part that led to his experimentation with avant-garde modes of representation such as "onomatopoeia to suggest the deafening explosions of mortar shells and the other new weapons."

Jones, Dorothy B. "War without Glory." *The Quarterly of Film, Radio and Television,* vol. VIII (1953–1954): 273–289.

Discussing the uniqueness of the 1930 film version of *All Quiet on the Western Front,* as an unflinching portrait that addresses the collective agony of the war on society in the same episodic manner as the novel, Jones charts how the film, a far more objective rendition of the novel, departs from the sensitivity to be found in the book. While the first third of the film consists of alternating still and moving shots of the combatants, a shift occurs to provide a fuller view of the wounded and the dying, a change which is marked by a scene of solitary reflection in which Paul Bäumer hears the voice of his teacher extolling the virtues of war to his students. In the final analysis, Jones contends that the visual representation of *All Quiet on the Western Front* is more objective, graphic, and universal. "We see and hear not only the stabbing bayonets and the screaming shells; but we experience as well the tensions, the unbearable anxiety which precedes the battle, the unmasked brutality of killing, and finally the sense of loss and depression which comes in the wake of a war experience."

Liedloff, Helmut. "Two War Novels: A Critical Comparison." *Revue de Littérature Comparee*, vol. XLII, no. 3 (July–September, 1968): 390–406.

Contrasting *A Farewell to Arms* to *Im Westen nichts Neues*, Liedloff discusses many of the differences between the two classic novels with respect to symbolism, language, structure, characterization, and their respective treatment of war. Liedloff maintains that, while Remarque's novel is sparse in its use of symbols in comparison to Hemingway, *All Quiet* is far more specific in its treatment of the soldiers' psychological status. The author sees the text's main fault as the absence of conversational language in its early parts, though this perceived shortcoming is corrected further into the narrative. "[F]rom the point of view of technique, *Farewell* is superior although *Im Westen* shows substantial accomplishments in the same direction.... From the point of view of content *Im Westen* appears as a substantially more comprehensive war novel."

Murdoch, Brian. "All Quiet on the Trojan Front: Remarque, Homer and War as the Targets of Literary Parody." *German Life and Letters*, vol. 43, no. 1 (October 1989): 49–62.

Focusing on *Vor Troja nichts Neues* (1930), a parody of *All Quiet* presumably written by Max Joseph Wolff, Murdoch contends that *Vor Troja* uses Remarque's novel to comment on Homer and, further, is evidence that *All Quiet* had achieved worldwide recognition. Murdoch argues that an understanding of the narrator in *Vor Troja*, who resembles Thersites, a common soldier in the *Iliad* whom Homer describes unfavorably, is the key to understanding Wolff's commentary on Remarque. "Wolff's book, though, also uses the externals and the context of Remarque's work to provide a basis for a reversal of the heroic ideals in Homer. Anachronism is a useful comic device. . . . *Vor Troja nichts Neues* attacks Ullstein's marketing strategy, mocks specific and easily identified elements of Remarque's narrative, and may also have been aimed at his pacifism."

————. "From the Frog's Perspective: *Im Westen nichts Neues* and *Der Weg zurück*." *The Novels of Erich Maria Remarque: Sparks of Life* (2006): 31–65.

Discussing the singular success of *All Quiet on the Western Front* in an international context, Murdoch identifies those aspects of the novel that contributed to its universal appeal, while responding to those early critics who argued that Remarque's use of a single narrator could not provide a valid representation of World War I. Among the attributes that Murdoch offers to address these critics are the absence of a precise chronology of events that would create another level of critical questioning, and the almost exclusive use of a single person narrator in the figure of the very young Paul Bäumer whose commentary, for the most part, always includes his comrades by referring to his company "we." Furthermore, as Murdoch points out, as casualties mount and Bäumer loses one friend after another, the reference to "we" is also tragically diminished until *All Quiet* reaches down to the individual. "Remarque reduces the *wir* element gradually throughout the work in parallel to what was a war of attrition that ultimately reached the single individual, when at the end Paul Bäumer is not just left alone, but is thrown onto his own inner resources without support from any side."

————. "Innocent Killing: Erich Maria Remarque and the Weimar Anti-War Novels." *German Studies in the Post-Holocaust Age* (2006): 141–168.

Evaluating Remarque as a Weimar novelist, Murdoch maintains that *All Quiet on the Western Front* and *The Way Back* need to be read as companion pieces reflecting on World War I and its immediate aftermath just before Hitler's election to power. Murdoch contends that the simplicity of plot, the journalistic mode of storytelling and the limited description of characters are deceptive, for *All Quiet* is a work in which Remarque has skillfully crafted a universal appeal and applicability of wartime experience. "There will probably be no more wars in the trenches, but the betrayal of one generation by another, the arbitrariness in the way in which wars begin, and the fact that much of the fighting is done by the uncomprehending young— these are lasting themes."

Schwarz, Wilhelm J. "The Works of Ernst Jünger and Erich Maria Remarque on World War I." *War and the Mind of Germany I.* Frankfurt/M." Peter Lang (1975): 17–32.

Contrasting *All Quiet on the Western Front* as a "memorial to the unknown soldier" to Ernst Jünger's war diary of World War I, *The Storm of Steel (In Stahlgewittern)*, which in idealizing war and the nobility of dying for the fatherland presents it as an epic, Schwarz provides a thoroughgoing catalog of the major themes of Remarque's novel, including the notion of bravery which he maintains is present in the sheer struggle to survive as well as in the young recruits who fight without training or experience. For all of the tragedy in *All Quiet on the Western Front*, Schwarz acknowledges that the camaraderie of the soldiers is ennobling and becomes the indispensable source of bravery within the novel. "Paul Bäumer, by himself, is just a nameless soldier in a great army. . . . But with his comrades Kropp and Kat beside him he is ready to defend this little spark of life that is his against a world that has gone biserk."

Wagener, Hans. *"All Quiet on the Western Front." Understanding Erich Maria Remarque* (1991): 9–37.

Using Remarque's prefatorial comments on *All Quiet*, that his book is "neither an accusation nor a confession," Wagener argues that though it purports simply to relate events that took place, it is also, simultaneously, Remarque's disclaimer regarding precise autobiographical reference to his own experience of World War I. Wagener's essay provides a chapter-by-chapter examination of the various issues surrounding Remarque's military service and comments on their fictional representation in *All Quiet* and concludes that this work, narrated by an ordinary soldier on the front lines, presents a variation within the genre of war novels and presages the direction of Remarque's literary endeavors. *"With All Quiet on the Western Front* he had found the basic theme for all his later literary works—life threatened by large, overbearing situations, whether they be political forces or deadly diseases. In all his future works the backgrounds change, but the basic underlying principle remains the same."

Contributors

Harold Bloom is Sterling Professor of the Humanities at Yale University. He is the author of 30 books, including *Shelley's Mythmaking, The Visionary Company, Blake's Apocalypse, Yeats, A Map of Misreading, Kabbalah and Criticism, Agon: Toward a Theory of Revisionism, The American Religion, The Western Canon,* and *Omens of Millennium: The Gnosis of Angels, Dreams, and Resurrection. The Anxiety of Influence* sets forth Professor Bloom's provocative theory of the literary relationships between the great writers and their predecessors. His most recent books include *Shakespeare: The Invention of the Human,* a 1998 National Book Award finalist, *How to Read and Why, Genius: A Mosaic of One Hundred Exemplary Creative Minds, Hamlet: Poem Unlimited, Where Shall Wisdom Be Found?,* and *Jesus and Yahweh: The Names Divine.* In 1999, Professor Bloom received the prestigious American Academy of Arts and Letters Gold Medal for Criticism. He has also received the International Prize of Catalonia, the Alfonso Reyes Prize of Mexico, and the Hans Christian Andersen Bicentennial Prize of Denmark.

Brian Murdoch has been a professor of German at the University of Stirling, Scotland. He is the author of *The Medieval Popular Bible: Expansions of Genesis in the Middle Ages* (2003), *Adam's Grace: Fall and Redemption in Medieval Literature* (2000), and *The Germanic Hero: Politics and Pragmatism in Early Medieval Poetry* (1996).

A.F. Bance has been a professor at the University of St. Andrews. He is the author of *Theodor Fontane: The Major Novels* (1982), "The Intellectual and the Crisis of Weimar: Heinrich Mann's Kobes," and translator of *The True Face of William Shakespeare: The Poet's Death Mask and Likenesses from Three Periods of His Life* by Hildegard Hammerschmidt-Hummel (2006).

Chris Daley is the author of "The 'Atrocious Privilege': Bearing Witness to War and Atrocity in O'Brien, Levi, and Remarque" (2005).

Hildegard Emmel is the author of *Weltklage und Bild der Welt in der Dichtung Goethes* (1957), *Das Gericht in der deutschen Literatur des 20. Jahrhunderts* (1963), and "Goethes Laune des Verliebten under der Mythos von Arkadien" (1956).

Vita Fortunati has been a professor of English literature at the University of Bologna. She is coeditor of the *Dictionary of Literary Utopias* (2000), an editor of *Travel Writing and the Female Imaginary* (2001), and coeditor of *Ford Maddox Ford and the Republic of Letters* (2002).

Dorothy B. Jones served as chief of the film reviewing and analysis section of OWI during World War II, in addition to having made a two-year study of Warner Brothers films for Jack Warner and received a two-year fellowship in film criticism from the Rockefeller Foundation. She is the author of "'Sunrise': A Murnau Masterpiece" (1955), "William Faulkner: Novel Into Film" (1953), and "The Language of Our Time" (1955).

Helmut Liedloff is professor emeritus at Southern Illinois University. He is the author of *Steinbeck in German Tanslation: A Study of Translational Practices* (1965) and coauthor with Jack Moeller of *Deutsch Heute: Grundstufe* (1988).

Alfredo Bonadeo is professor emeritus of Italian literature at the University of California, Santa Barbara. He is the author of *D'Annunzio and the Great War* (1995), *Mark of the Beast: Death and Degradation in the Literature of the Great War* (1989), and *L'Italia e gl'Italiani nell'immaginazione romantica inglese: Lord Byron, John Ruskin, D.H. Lawrence* (1984).

Modris Eksteins has been a professor of history at the University of Toronto. He is the author of *Walking Since Daybreak: A Story of*

Eastern Europe, World War II, and the Heart of our Century (1999), *The Limits of Reason: The German Democratic Press and the Collapse of Weimar Democracy* (1975), and coeditor of *Nineteenth-century Germany: A Symposium* (1983).

Hans Wagener has been a professor of German literature at the University of California, Santa Barbara. He is the author of *Robert Neumann: Biographie* (2007), *Carl Zuckmayer Criticism: Tracing Endangered Fame* (1995), and *Understanding Franz Werfel* (1993).

Robert Baird has been a professor in the English department at the University of Illinois where he has taught film. His research and writing have focused on the psychology of visual spectatorship.

Wilhelm J. Schwarz is the author of *Conversations with Peter Rosei* (1994), *Der Erzähler Siegfried Lenz* (1974) and *Heinrich Böll, Teller of Tales; A Study of His Works and Characters* (1969).

Acknowledgments

Brian Murdoch, from "From the Frog's Perspective," originally published in *The Novels of Erich Maria Remarque: Sparks of Life*, Rochester, NY: Camden House, 2006. Used by permission.

Brian Murdoch, from "All Quiet on the Trojan Front: Remarque, Homer and War as the Targets of Literary Parody," *German Life and Letters*, 43:1, October 1989, Basil Blackwell. Used by permission.

A.F. Bance, from "'Im Westen Nichts Neues': A Bestseller in Context," from *The Modern Language Review*, vol. 72, no. 1 (January 1977). © Modern Humanities Research Association.

Chris Daley, from "The 'Atrocious Privilege,'" *Arms and the Self: War, the Military, and Autobiographical Writing*, Alex Vernon, ed. © 2005 by the Kent State University Press.

Hildegard Emmel, from "The Novel during the Weimar Republic," *History of the German Novel*, Wayne State University Press, 1984.

Vita Fortunati, from "The Impact of the First World War on Private Lives," *History and Representation in Ford Madox Ford's Writings*, International Ford Madox Ford Studies, Rodopi, 2004. Used by permission.

Dorothy B. Jones, from "War without Glory," *The Quarterly of Film Radio and Television*, vol. VIII: 1953–1954, University of California Press.

Helmut Liedloff, from " Two War Novels: A Critical Comparison" *Revue de Littérateur Comparée*, vol. 42, no. 3 (July–September 1968).

Index